KT-197-614

BERLITZ®

JAPAN

How to use our guide

These 256 pages cover the **highlights** of Japan, grouped by area under seven different headings. Although not exhaustive, our selection of sights will enable you to make the most of your holiday.

The **sights** to see are contained between pages 59 and 185. Those most highly recommended are pinpointed by the Berlitz traveller symbol.

The **Where to Go** section on page 53 will help you plan your visit according to the time available.

For **general background** see the sections Japan and the Japanese (p. 8), Historical Landmarks (p. 18), Facts and Figures (p. 20) and History (p. 21).

Entertainment and **activities** (including eating out) are described between pages 185 and 217.

The **practical information,** hints and tips you will need before and during your trip begin on page 218. This section is arranged alphabetically with a list for easy reference.

The **map section** at the back of the book (pp. 244–252) will help you find your way round and locate the principal sights.

Finally, if there is anything you cannot find, look in the complete **index** (pp. 253–256).

8th Edition (1994/1995)

CONTENTS

CONTENTS

Text:	Jack Altman
Staff Editor:	Christina Jackson
Photography:	Claude Huber; Tony Stone Associates, London, pp. 183, 188
Layout:	Doris Haldemann
Cartography:	🅕 Falk-Verlag, Hamburg

Acknowledgements
We wish to express our warmest thanks to the Japan National Tourist Organization in Tokyo, in particular to Mr Takashi Nagaoka, to Mr Ishii of the Japan National Tourist Organization in Geneva, and to Japan Air Lines for their help and cooperation in the preparation of this guide. We are also grateful to Mrs Akiko Barbier for her assistance.

Although we make every effort to ensure the accuracy of all the information in this book, changes occur incessantly. We cannot therefore take responsibility for facts, prices, addresses and circumstances in general that are constantly subject to alteration. Our guides are updated on a regular basis as we reprint, and we are always grateful to readers who let us know of any errors, changes or serious omissions they come across.

CHINA

DEMOCRATIC PEOPLE'S
REPUBLIC OF KOREA

REPUBLIC
OF KOREA

S E A O

O H N

Tsushima Is. *Oki Is.*

Matsue

Yonago

Taka
Kanazawa

Shimonoseki
Kitakyushu
Yamaguchi Hiroshima Tsuyama Tottori
Iwakuni Fukui
Fukuoka Ube Fukuyama Okayama
Saga Kure Himeji **Kyoto** Gifu
Kurume Onomichi Kurashiki Itami
Nagasaki Usa Imabari Niihama Takamatsu **Kobe** Otsu Nag
Shimabara Beppu Matsuyama **Osaka** Nara Oka.
Oita Tsu Tokaichi
Kumamoto Uwajima Kochi Tokushima Ise
Yatsushiro Wakayama Toyohashi
Hamama

Nobeoka
Kagoshima *Shikoku* C. Muroto
Miyazaki C. Ashizuri
Ibusuki C. Shiono
Kyushu
C. Sata C. Toi

OKINAWA

P A C I F I C

JAPAN AND THE JAPANESE

Whiz around the country in their super-express "bullet train", the *shinkansen,* and you can't help believing that the Japanese are determined to get to the 21st century before the rest of us. One look at the formidable megalopolis stretching from Tokyo south-west along the Pacific coast, and you may well feel that they've already arrived.

The train glides past the gigantic industrial installations around Yokohama Harbour, through sprawling factory towns like Nagoya, creeping in on the temples and palaces of the old imperial capital of Kyoto, to the great commercial, concrete, steel and glass skyscraper jungle of

Osaka. Some 50 million people, more than one in three of the total population, live in this 300-mile (500-km.)-long urban belt, heart of the trading and manufacturing machine that has captured the world's imagination.

But, through the train window, you can also catch your first glimpse of the country's most haunting image: the sacred snow-capped volcano of Mt. Fuji, symbol of that other, mythic Japan beyond mere technology.

Outside the megalopolis and even well within its confines, you can wander in the tranquillity of brilliant green moss-covered temple gardens or sit quietly on woven-reed *tatami* floors in a

Two Japanese moods: festive joy or a Kyoto temple's serenity.

restaurant alcove shielded from other guests by *shoji* latticed paper screens, and suddenly you float in a Japan of another age.

And even further away, beyond the coastal plains and into the rugged mountains, you'll find yourself in a land of dense virgin forest and occasional rushing torrents that seems untouched by any human history at all, a truly primeval world knowing nothing of Sony transistors and Hitachi videos, Honda motorcycles and Mitsubishi oil tankers.

Yet it would be wrong to think of these worlds as totally distinct compartments. The Japanese themselves wander easily from one to the other. The director of a computer company who wears a business suit in downtown Tokyo is quite likely to change back home into a kimono, the traditional Japanese costume for both men and women. Even the younger generation, strutting in leather jacket, tee shirt and blue jeans or whatever other street fashion currently commands their fancy, will now and then reveal with a bow or other gesture of deference to their elders that old values have not totally lost their hold. Militant political activists hand out their revolutionary tracts at street corners with a gentle grace that would do honour to a master of the centuries-old tea ceremony.

You'll witness this constant interaction of past and present at Ise-Shima, most revered of all Japanese sanctuaries. Celebrating Japan's association with the Sun Goddess and her grandson, God of the Earth, this sanctuary was established some 1,700 years ago, but the principal shrine you'll see today was built in 1973. Unlike Christianity's massive Gothic cathedrals, seemingly built for eternity, this austere wooden structure is dismantled every 20 years and replaced by a new one. The deities of Japan's national Shinto religion are felt to be present in the eternity of the natural surroundings, in this case a beautiful forest of cedars. The man-made shrine is just there for the fleeting present.

This strong sense that the Japanese people have of the transient quality of life is doubtless in part an inevitable response to their country's geography. It's a highly volatile piece of the earth's crust, pock-marked with many volcanoes and regularly subject to earthquakes. And typhoons. Over the ages, drawing on the apparently inexhaustible resources of their forests, they built everything of wood, monumental and residential building alike, and waited

Tokyo's Ginza brings the old and new worlds together.

fatalistically for them to burn down, collapse or be swept away in one catastrophe or another—and then set about rebuilding. It wasn't until a 20th-century Western architect, Frank Lloyd Wright, came to Tokyo to build a new earthquake-resistant Imperial Hotel that it was seriously considered desirable to withstand the ravages of nature.

Today, office and apartment buildings are of course constructed with modern materials. But the ideal home, despite the prevailing obsession with electronic gadgetry and all the latest technology, is still the traditional, simple and oh-so-elegant house of wooden walls and paper sliding partitions, air-conditioned, perhaps, but all as nicely combustible as ever.

Japan consists of four main islands, dominated by Honshu, on which Tokyo is located, with Hokkaido to the north, Shikoku across the narrow Inland Sea and Kyushu to the south-west. With over 3,900 smaller islands, the Japanese archipelago, from north-east to south-west, would stretch neatly from Montreal down to Miami. The climate correspondingly varies from the snowy northern tip of Hokkaido to the subtropical parts of southern Kyushu and Okinawa. Honshu benefits from a healthy, temperate climate. Winters are marked by heavy snows along the north-western coast facing the Sea of Japan, but they're more mild and sunny on the Pacific coast, permitting a double crop of the all-important rice staple.

The frequent rain throughout the year ought to have been an agricultural boon, but the jagged mountain ranges and impenetrable forests leave less than one-fifth of the country suitable for habitation and farming. Despite a total land surface larger than that of East and West Germany put together, Japan's 120 millions have to crowd into the coastal plains and narrow river valleys. In terms of the ratio between population and usable land, Japan is the most densely populated country in the world.

This tremendous population density explains many phenomena that initially astonish Westerners: the famous "people-pushers" who squeeze passengers into the rush-hour trains at Tokyo's Shinjuku subway station; the staggering traffic jams despite the stacking of expressways one on top of the other to move even more cars in and out of the city; the new "capsule hotels" packing the maximum number of guests into tiny narrow berths one on top of the other like baggage lockers. And it also explains, to some extent, the people's usually exquisite politeness, chosen as the best way to survive even when piled one on top of the other.

Japanese politeness and self-discipline have become a legend for our times. Visitors stand amazed at the harmony that reigns amid the bustle of city life, the absence of the kind of street violence that has become endemic in crowded cities elsewhere in the world. American and European managers look with wistful admiration at the organization of Japanese factories.

Historians and sociologists like to explain it all as a continuation of the feudal spirit of the past, seeing company presidents as latter-day shoguns and middle management as recycled samurai. It's argued that the warriors' age-old communal training in the martial arts has been replaced by corporate calisthenics in the factory front yard. Whether such theories and parallels are valid or not, it is clear that the prevailing social harmony owes much to the homogeneity of the Japanese population. Peopled originally by Mongolian, Chinese, Korean and perhaps also Malayan settlers, the country has had several thousand years to form a solid ethnic unity. Japan was not subject to the kind of large scale immigration or—until the United States occupation in 1945—foreign invasion that has made for social conflict in other countries.

But this does not mean Japanese society has remained totally free of social discrimination. The country's 670,000 Koreans, many of them installed in Japan for two or more generations, regularly protest their second-class status. The Ainu, an ethnically distinct community regarded by anthropologists as the islands' original settlers and now grouped almost exclusively in Hokkaido, campaign for civil rights in a movement similar to that of the Indians or blacks in the United States. A third group, not of different ethnic origin from the Japanese mainstream but unmistakably inferior in status, is formed by the *burakumin* (literally "village dwellers", a euphemistic substitute for their old caste name *eta,* "much filth", abolished at the end of the 19th century). They are descendants of outcasts employed for the originally taboo, and still despised, trades of butchery, leather-work and handling of corpses, and live in separate hamlets or on city outskirts—400,000 in Tokyo and an estimated 3 million throughout the country. You're most likely to come across them cleaning up garbage in parks and temple grounds or shining shoes at railway stations. After years of inertia, prompted perhaps more by embarrassment than indifference, the Japanese government is responding to the

13

demands of these "outsiders" for better treatment.

Traditional Japanese values have been considerably shaken up in the 20th century. The Western way of life has proved seductive (though the Walkman may have been just the beginning of Nippon's revenge). But there's still something specifically Japanese about the way Western ideas are adapted—a mistake to think they're just slavishly copied—for Japanese needs. For centuries, the Japanese national spirit, known as *yamato damashii,* embodied in its best sense the courage, tact, loyalty, endurance and affection expected of every good Japanese. It was held in the same high esteem as, say, the "frontier spirit" of the Americans or the "esprit gaulois" of the French and achieved its most heroic expression among the proud sam-

urai. The militarist regime of the 1930s invoked the concept to prepare the country for war and convince the people of their innate superiority over the enemy. The subsequent disillusionment has tended to discredit *yamato damashii* as a desirable ideal for many of today's younger generation. But many people feel that the true spirit of *yamato damashii* has lived on as the unnamed driving force behind the management

Even in crowded Japan, you can find a deserted beach—almost.

methods and worker efficiency of the spectacular postwar recovery. The question remains as to whether the essentially collective values of traditional Japan can continue to appeal to the new generations demanding more individualism.

The clash of modern and tra-

15

ditional values leads to some puzzling, sometimes infuriating, but always fascinating contradictions along your sightseeing route. The Shinto religion attributes a divine quality to all kinds of natural phenomena: mountains, trees, rivers, or strangely shaped rocks along the rugged coasts. In turn, the Buddhist tradition has taught a reverence for landscape at an aesthetic level that few other civilizations can match. As in centuries past, the people go on mass pilgrimages to witness the springtime blossoming of the cherry trees, or the golds, reds and coppers of the autumn maples. But they don't seem to mind the calm being shattered by disco music blaring from loudspeakers hidden in the trees to "entertain" the visitors. Beautifully landscaped parks and gardens, even within hallowed temple grounds, may be dotted with garish souvenir shops, to which admirers of the perfect perspectives have to learn to turn a blind eye.

If you think the fanatical following accorded baseball suggests that Japanese society is hopelessly Americanized, just see what happens when a 15-day sumo wrestling tournament comes to town. The centuries-old ceremony and ritual prove more than a match for the razzmatazz of the great American game. On television, a home-run by the Yomiuri Giants or Seibu Lions is an occasion for fireworks, but the slow-motion instant replay of two 300-pound sumo champions hurling each other across the ring with an *utchari* backward-pivot throw can be a moment of poetic ecstasy.

Businessmen who rule their companies by day with iron discipline and austere self-control can be seen in nightclubs giggling over many, many glasses of whisky or *sake* and singing versions of Frank Sinatra's "I did it my way". Their employees may have spent their day wielding precision instruments to turn out cars, cameras or can-openers that will continue undercutting the world's markets. After work, you can see them playing, glassy-eyed, with a *pachinko* pinball machine, manipulating hundreds of little metal balls going nowhere. Back home, wives who may at first seem passive and subservient are formidably powerful mothers driving their children to scholastic success.

And over this amazing nation presides Emperor Akihito, whose father was, until 1946, treated as a divinity. He performs a symbolic function not dissimilar to that of modern European monarchs, but remains largely out of sight, shrouded in mistery.

Japan itself is a magnificent

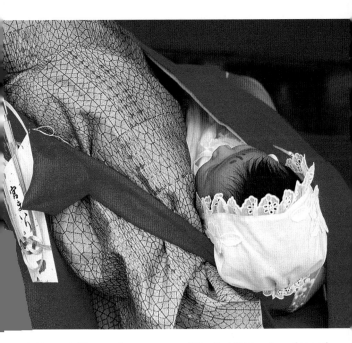

Babies carried in a pouch get a different perspective on life.

mystery and, like a magician's trick, it would spoil the pleasure if someone explained it to you. Don't worry, everyone tries but nobody can—not even, it seems, the Japanese themselves. Just look around and listen. Taste the delicate food, take in the formal beauties of *kabuki* theatre,

of Zen Buddhist rock gardens, of *ikebana* flower arrangement, if such is your taste, participate in the graceful tea ceremony or watch the redoubtable *kendo*, fencing with staves. Set them alongside your teeming impressions of that headlong rush into the next century. If they do get there before us, you can at least say, even if you don't understand how they did it, that you watched them go.

HISTORICAL LANDMARKS

Jomon Culture c. 10,000– 250 B.C.		Pit-dwellers live from hunting, fishing and gathering of roots and nuts.
	660 B.C.	Legendary date of founding of imperial dynasty.
Yayoi Culture c. 250 B.C.– 300 A.D.		The techniques of wheel-made pottery and wet cultivation of rice arrive from China and Korea.
Yamato Period c. 300–710	c. 300	Unification of Japan, with Yamato Court as nucleus. Period of Chinese influence.
	c. 538	Introduction of Buddhism from China. Rise to power of Soga family.
	645	Sogas ousted by Nakatomi Kamatari, founder of Fujiwara dynasty.
Nara Period 710–784	710	Imperial Court established at Nara.
Heian Period 794–1185	794	Imperial Court moved to Heian-kyo.
	1156	Four-year war between Taira and Minamoto clans.
	1185	Battle of Dannoura; Minamotos prevail.
Kamakura Period 1192–1333	1192	Yoritomo Minamoto becomes first shogun.
	1274/1281	Two unsuccessful Mongol invasions under Kublai Khan.
	1333	Fall of Kamakura *bakufu*.
Muromachi Period 1338–1573	1339–1573	Shogunate of Ashikaga family.
	1467–1568	Civil war between provincial *daimyo*.
	1543	Arrival of Portuguese explorers.

	1549	Francis Xavier lands at Kagoshima.
	1568	Rise to power of Nobunaga, Hideyoshi and Tokugawa.
Momoyama Period 1573–1600	1582	Nobunaga assassinated; Hideyoshi succeeds him.
	1587	Persecution of Christians begins.
	1592	Hideyoshi launches attack on Korea and China but is repulsed.
	1598	Death of Hideyoshi; Tokugawa seizes power.
Edo Period 1603–1867	1603	Ieyasu Tokugawa takes title of shogun. Capital established at Edo.
	1635	Isolation of Japan from rest of world begins.
	1854	Treaty of Kanagawa opens up Japan to trade with U.S.
Meiji Restoration 1868–1912	1868	Emperor Meiji comes to throne. Imperial power restored.
	1894–5	Sino-Japanese War.
	1904–5	Russo-Japanese War.
Modern Times 1912–	1937	Japan declares war on Chinese Nationalists.
	1940	Japan joins Axis powers in World War II.
	1941	Japan bombs Pearl Harbor.
	1945	Hiroshima and Nagasaki bombed; Japan surrenders.
	1945–52	United States occupation.
	1952–1993	Rapid industrialization brings Japan to forefront of world affairs.
	1989	Death of Emperor Hirohito. Akihito succeeds to the throne.

FACTS AND FIGURES

Geography: The Japanese archipelago lies off the north-east coast of Asia. It consists of four main islands—from north-east to south-west, Hokkaido, Honshu, Shikoku and Kyushu—and over 3,900 smaller islands. Covering a surface area of 147,200 sq. mi. (377,728 sq. km.), the country ranks 42nd in the world in geographical size but 7th in population. With the Sea of Japan to the west and the Pacific Ocean to the east, the islands describe an arc 1,700 mi. (2,800 km.) long, the closest point to the Asian continent being 100 mi. (160 km.) across the Straits of Tsushima to South Korea. Mountains cover 72% of the land leaving only 18% flat enough and free of dense forest for farming and habitation. Highest point: Mt. Fuji, at 12,388 feet (3,776 m.).

Population: 120 million, plus 670,000 Koreans and 130,000 other non-Japanese. Density is 316 per sq. km.

Capital: Tokyo (pop. inner metropolitan area 8,330,000).

Major cities: Yokohama (2,900,000), Osaka (2,700,000), Nagoya (2,100,000), Kyoto (1,500,000), Sapporo (1,500,000), Kobe (1,400,000), Fukuoka (1,100,000), Kita-Kyushu (1,100,000), Kawasaki (1,000,000), Hiroshima (900,000).

Government: Japan is a parliamentary democracy. Under the Constitution of 1947, the emperor is titular head of a state in which sovereignty rests with the people and their elected representatives, headed by a prime minister and his cabinet. Parliament is known as the Diet, comprising a House of Representatives (511 seats) and House of Councillors (252 seats). The country is divided into 47 prefectures, each with a governor.

Religion: Shinto is the indigenous cult open to all citizens, who may combine it with Buddhism (83 million adherents), Christianity (880,000) or Islam (155,000).

HISTORY

When it comes to mixing myth and history in telling the story of their country's origins, the Japanese make less bones about it than Westerners do. According to the earliest official Japanese accounts, the 8th-century *Kojiki (Record of Ancient Matters)* and *Nihon-shoki (Chronicles of Japan),* the islands of Japan were born of a marriage between the god Izanagi and his sister Izanami. They also, but only later, gave birth to the sun, in the form of the goddess Amaterasu, who endowed the Japanese imperial family with its regalia of bronze mirror, iron sword and jewel (the mirror is kept to this day at the Shinto shrine of Ise-Shima).

Before you dismiss all this as the "mere myth" of Japan's misty Dark Ages, it's as well to remember that the Japanese continued to trace the imperial dynasty directly back to those deities until Emperor Hirohito's New Year message in 1946 denounced "the false conception that the emperor is divine". Many followed Japan's best-known novelist Yukio Mishima* in deploring this formal break

---

* Only recently have the Japanese adopted the Western style of placing the family name, e.g. Mishima, after the given name, in this case Yukio. To avoid confusion, we have applied the Western style throughout.

with tradition, and the creation myth has persisted in the popular imagination, side by side with more scientific versions of Japan's origins.

For those who prefer to stick to the bones—the bones and weapons and pottery most recently uncovered by archaeologists—the oriental equivalent of Neanderthal Man crossed a since submerged land bridge from eastern Siberia to what is now Sakhalin Island and northern Japan some 100,000 years ago. These ancestors of the present-day Ainu, whose Caucasoid facial and body hair distinguished them from subsequent Mongoloid immigrants from China, Manchuria, Korea and perhaps Malaya, originally settled throughout the Japanese archipelago. (It was the growth and military assertion of the newcomers that drove the "hairy people", as they were labelled, back north to their present concentration in Hokkaido.)

The oldest Stone Age settlements to be discovered (10,000 B.C.) are known as Jomon, "cord pattern", after the style of their handmade pottery—among the earliest to be found anywhere in the world and of rich and imaginative design. Its makers dwelled in sunken pits and lived from hunting, fishing and the gathering of roots and nuts. It wasn't until the 3rd century B.C.

that techniques of rice cultivation (and wheel-made pottery) arrived from Korea, along with irrigation methods that are still in use today.

The scarcity of flatlands suitable for cultivation made it possible for a small aristocratic elite to gain quick control of the food resources. This set the pattern of hierarchic rule that was to prevail right up to the last half of the 19th century (some would claim, in economic terms at least, that it still persists today).

Lacking its own natural resources, Japan at first had access to just enough bronze and iron from Korea for Chinese-style mirrors and fragile weapons and bells that were necessarily symbolic rather than functional. By A.D. 300 there was sufficient iron for agricultural implements. The thatched houses built on stilts were much the same as some of the farmhouses you see today away from the main population centres. You can also see in many country graveyards, figurines of men, animals and houses similar to the *haniwa,* modelled ceramic cylinders used in decorating the tombs of this prehistoric culture.

We say "prehistoric" because there are no reliable accounts of this period—though 3rd-century Chinese documents speak of a Japanese priestess-queen Himiko ruling over a land of law-abiding

people who enjoyed alcoholic drink and were divided into classes distinguished by tattoo marks. Five centuries later, Japan's own *Kojiki* and *Nihonshoki* chronicles tell how the imperial dynasty was created in the year 660 B.C., when the first emperor, Jimmu ("Divine Warrior"), great grandson of the Sun Goddess's grandson, embarked on an expedition of conquest from Kyushu along the Inland Sea coast to the Yamato plain of the Kinki region (surrounding modern Osaka and Kyoto).

Plausible chronicling, laced with a healthy dose of mythology, begins with the arrival of Korean scribes at the Japanese

court around A.D. 400, at a time when Japan also had a military foothold in southern Korea. The state of Yamato, as early Japan was known, was organized into *uji* or clusters of clans, with subordinate guilds of farmers, fishermen, hunters, weavers and potters, all subject to the dominant *uji* of the imperial family.

Chinese Influence

The Koreans forced the Japanese out of their peninsula in the 6th century, but not before they had made a present to the Yamato court of the sacred images and scriptures of Chinese Buddhism.

Just as Christianity carried Mediterranean culture to north-

Shinto "way of the gods" unites Japanese with their ancestors.

ern Europe, so Buddhism brought Chinese culture into Japanese society. Throughout the 7th and 8th centuries, monks, scholars and artists made the perilous trip across the Sea of Japan to study Chinese religion, history, music, literature and painting.

An outstanding figure of this time was Prince Shotoku, who in 604 developed the "Seventeen Article Constitution" outlining a code of human conduct and the ideals of state, which provided a basic law for the nation. He also

Way of the Gods

The major tenet of Japan's indigenous cult of Shinto was the imperial family's direct descent from the Sun Goddess, thus establishing the divinity of the emperor. For this reason the emperor has always been the titular head of the cult, with a priestly function (his divinity being renounced only in 1946).

Literally "the way of the gods", Shinto is a form of nature-worship, with shrines in places of great natural beauty such as mountain tops or forests, where divine spirits are felt to be present in waterfalls, unusual rocks or great trees. Lacking the kind of philosophy or moral code conventionally associated with other great world religions, Shinto insists mainly on respect for the deities being shown by ritual purity. Menstruation, childbirth, sickness, injury and death are all considered sources of impurity—so that workers in slaughterhouses, leather tanneries or graveyards have traditionally been restricted to a caste of "untouchables", known today as the burakumin.

The numerous purification ceremonies include rinsing the mouth at a water-trough when approaching a shrine; priests waving sacred branches over the faithful; and sumo wrestlers tossing a handful of salt across the ring before combat begins. This concern for purification may also explain the enduring attachment of the Japanese to their hot spring spas and the piping hot water of their wooden bathtubs.

In a country where people see no internal contradiction in having a Christian baptism, Shinto wedding and Buddhist burial because they happen to like the aesthetics of the various ceremonies, Shinto remains a much less solemn cult than Westerners are used to. Typically, the commercial bustle around the shrine at Tokyo's Asakusa evokes the atmosphere of a Western country fair. In front of the shrine, people clap their hands to attract the gods' attention, bow respectfully, toss some coins into a slotted box and offer up a prayer. Then they go off to the food stalls, amusement booths and souvenir shops, all located inside the sanctuary grounds.

established relations with the Sui dynasty in China. Through him, the imperial court developed Chinese patterns of centralized government, with its formal bureaucracy of eight court ranks. The Chinese calendar was used to calculate the year of Japan's foundation by counting back the 1,260 years of the Chinese cosmological cycle. The answer: 660 B.C., still the official date celebrated nationwide.

Already at this early stage in its history, Japan was for the most part only nominally ruled by the emperor. De facto power was exercised by the militarily and economically strongest family. The Sogas had promoted Buddhism as an imperially sanctioned counterweight to Shinto, along with the new-fangled Chinese customs, to weaken the influence of their more conservative rivals. But they in turn were ousted in A.D. 645 by Nakatomi Kamatari, founder of the great Fujiwara clan which was to rule Japanese affairs for several hundred years and still provide prominent advisers to the emperor up to the 19th century.

It was under the guidance of Kamatari that the Emperor Tenchi implemented the Taika Reforms to streamline centralized government, impose Chinese-style taxation (by household unit), conduct a census of the national population and draw up the country's first law codes. With a pragmatism that was to become the hallmark of Japan's borrowings from other civilizations right up to the present day, the Taika Reforms adapted the model of China's Tang dynasty (A.D. 618–907) to specifically Japanese traditions. For instance, the Chinese principle of a meritocracy through training all the best available talents had to yield to Japanese class distinctions, which restricted the new Chinese-style university education to sons of the aristocracy.

The Nara Period

One of the new ideas was to set up a permanent residential capital for the imperial court, initially at Naniwa (present-day Osaka) and then a little to the east, at Nara, in 710. The site was chosen by experts in geomancy, with proper regard for the spiritually favourable location of surrounding hills, woodland and streams. Modern visitors will not scoff at this age-old concern with harmonious landscape.

Laid out like a chessboard (almost half the size of China's similarly designed capital Chang'an), Nara had its imperial palace at the northern end, with the tile-roofed court residences, Buddhist monasteries and cedar-wood Shinto shrines stretching out to the south. In those peaceful years without the threat of foreign invasion or civil war, there were no city ramparts. The entrenched aristocracy was unassailed.

The era known as the Nara Period was characterized by the religious fervour of the Buddhist monks and the accompanying artistic achievements. The Japanese were attracted more to Buddhism's ritual and art than to its complex philosophy, rendered all the more difficult because its texts were, for several centuries, available only in Chinese, the language of a small court elite.

25

Buddhist monks brought great progress in Japanese architecture, bronze-casting, bridge-building and sculpture. To this day, historians of Chinese art find the best surviving examples of Tang-dynasty architecture among the 7th- and 8th-century temples in and around Nara.

By marrying his daughters to sons of the reigning emperor and then engineering timely abdications, a Fujiwara contrived always to be father-in-law, uncle or grandfather behind the throne. Very often the emperor was only a minor, so that the Fujiwara patriarch acted as regent. He then persuaded the emperor to abdicate soon after his majority and the regency would continue for the next youthful incumbent. The important thing was to have the emperor's sanction for the regent's political decisions.

Very few emperors were reluctant to submit to Fujiwara domination. The burden of his spiritual functions as high priest of the Shinto cult and the tasks of administration led the emperor to welcome an early abdication, frequently to retire to a life of Buddhist meditation and scholarship. A rare and remarkable exception was the Empress Koken, a voluptuous

Buddha's teachings were brought to Nara from China.

and fervent Buddhist—not a contradiction at the Nara court. She defied the Fujiwaras, ordered the exile and quiet strangulation of their choice for the throne, her own grandson, and continued to wield considerable power in tandem with her lover, a fiery Buddhist monk named Dokyo.

When Koken died in 770, the Fujiwaras saw to it that a woman would never again hold the reins of power. Besides what they regarded as typically capricious female behaviour, the Fujiwaras resented the Buddhist clergy's great and growing influence in imperial affairs. There were too many monasteries in and around Nara. It was time to move the capital.

The Golden Heian Era

A first attempt to move was abandoned after ten years of calamities in the imperial family made it clear that the topography of the chosen site was not propitious. The geomancers went back to their drawing boards and in 794 came up with Heian-kyo, modern Kyoto, which remained the home of the imperial family until 1869.

The move to Heian-kyo brought with it a decrease in Chinese influence, in favour of purely Japanese national values. In theory, all lands belonged to the emperor, and the peasants who cultivated it paid a tax to the

27

government. However, over the years, grants of tax-free land had been made to Buddhist temples and members of the court aristocracy. Thus the most powerful families carved out for themselves whole regions that were to become the fiefdoms of Japanese feudalism.

By the end of the 8th century, the clans had created a hierarchy of *shiki* or rights from the highest to the lowest rank of society: the aristocrat or court patron lent his prestige to a powerful provincial proprietor, who employed a competent estate-manager to oversee smallholders, who worked their farms with dependent labourers. This structure of interdependent rights and obligations was to serve Japanese

---

Japanese Buddhism
The spiritual philosophy of Buddhism originated in India around 500 B.C. with the teachings of Siddhartha Gautama, the Indian prince who became Buddha (Sanskrit for "Enlightened One"). In the same way as Western monotheism divided into Judaism and Christianity, Buddhism split into two schools. Theravada, "Doctrine of the Elders", considered closer to the original teaching, is observed in Sri Lanka, Burma, Thailand and Cambodia, while Mahayana, the "Larger Vehicle", comparable in its ritual and social evolution to Christianity, is found in China, Korea and Japan.

Pure Buddhist doctrine teaches the quest for enlightenment, nirvana, by the progressive abandonment of desire, source of all life's pain. In Japan, partly because of the barrier of the Chinese language of the scriptures, but also because of a general resistance to metaphysical thought, Buddhist prac-

tice shifted away from private contemplation to public charity works, with celibacy and asceticism gradually being dropped.

For the Japanese, Buddhism initially appealed as a magical protector both for the state and for noble families, who built temples near their homes. New sects in the 9th century spread Buddhism throughout the country, and the religion evolved from protector of the aristocracy to popular vehicle of faith and hope for the common people, who were attracted by the incantations and elaborate ceremonial. By the 12th century, Buddhism had integrated successfully with the national cult of Shinto, along with those elements of Chinese Confucianism appropriate to the Japanese character —family solidarity, filial piety, loyalty to the ruler and to authority in general. As always, the Japanese were proving themselves not slavish imitators, but ingenious adaptors.

society right into the 20th century. (Many feel that, in the economic sphere at least, it has reasserted itself after the United States occupation's attempt to "democratize" the system. In place of court patrons, highly protective government ministries sponsor the big conglomerates [proprietors] who deploy the redoubtable company executives [estate-managers] to oversee factory managers [smallholders], with the great Japanese work force taking the place of the medieval dependent labourers.)

Meanwhile, Heian court life blossomed in an effusion of aesthetic expression. Princes and princesses judged the merits of birds, insects, flowers, roots or seashells. Literary party games held in ornate palace gardens required each guest to compose a small poem as his wine cup floated towards him along a miniature winding channel of water. Expeditions were organized to the best vantage points for the first spring cherry blossom, and special pavilions were built to watch the rising of the full moon.

Every gesture, from the most banal opening of an umbrella to the sublimest act of lovemaking, had its appropriate ceremonial. Conversation often took the form of elegant exchanges of improvised verse. Lest you think all this was unduly effete or decadent, it's as well to remember that the tougher feudal warlords who took over at the end of the Heian period incorporated many of these aesthetic elements into their austere daily lives. More than anything else, it was the Heian court that provided the enduring impetus for the courtesy of the 20th-century company director or for the awesomely graceful arrangements of food in a modern Japanese supermarket.

The changing role of Chinese culture in Japanese life was epitomized in the language itself. Having no indigenous alphabet, Japanese scholars had with the greatest difficulty tried to adapt the complex ideograms of monosyllabic Chinese to the essentially polysyllabic Japanese. They now developed a simplified, abbreviated set of *kana* characters more appropriate to Japanese.

But the cultivated gentlemen of the court continued to write in Chinese, which had the scholarly prestige of Latin in medieval Europe. It was left to the ladies to write in the more "frivolous" native tongue. And so it was the ladies who produced the first two masterpieces of Japanese literature. Around 1010, Shikibu Murasaki wrote *Genji Monogatari (The Tale of Genji),* a sophisticated psychological study of the amorous and other adventures of a Heian prince, the world's first real novel. *Makura-no-soshi*

29

(Pillow Book) is a lady-in-waiting's lively anecdotal account of court life. Both are written in everyday language with great style and elegance, contrasting with the stilted forms of the "old school" reserved for men.

But all was not wine and poems and cherry blossoms. With the proliferation of tax-free land-ownership in the remoter corners of the realm, local militias had to be enlisted to ward off roving brigands. As the richer families sought new land for cultivation, the armies were also used to drive the Ainu tribes further north.

The Minamoto and Taira families exploited this military activity to build provincial power bases independent of the central government at the Heian court. The armies had quickly become fully fledged feudal structures with *samurai* (retainers) and *bushi* (warriors) pledging a vassal's allegiance to their overlords. The families kept a firm foothold at court. The Minamoto clan was known as the "claws and teeth" of the Fujiwaras, too busy with administrative affairs and court intrigue to dirty their fingers with warfare. The Taira clan looked for their main chance by defending the interests of retired emperors.

After rival Fujiwara factions had been struggling for years to gain control of the imperial throne, they turned to the Taira and Minamoto armies in 1156 to wage the four-year war that heralded the end of the golden age of the Heian court. The Taira, controlling the region along the Inland Sea, defeated the Minamoto armies based in the Kanto province east of the capital.

A Fujiwara continued nominally as regent, but it was Kiyomori, lord of the Taira, who made the decisions. The dogs of war had become the masters. As the power behind the power behind the throne, Kiyomori, a tough but cultivated man, controlled the government from his palace in the capital. But his old Minamoto rivals pursued a grass-roots policy out in the provinces. Over the next 20 years, the Minamotos acquired new strength by offering better guarantees to local landowners—and their armies—than they could expect from court. A new offensive, the decisive Gempei War, was launched in 1180. Five years later the Taira were overthrown after defeat in the straits between western Honshu and Kyushu at the titanic sea battle of Dannoura, which has a place in Japanese annals comparable to Waterloo or Stalingrad.

Koryuji Temple exerted a major influence on Japan's rulers.

Enter the Shoguns

Japan's austere, ruthless but statesmanlike new ruler, Yoritomo Minamoto, set up his government well away from the "softening" influence of court life that had been the undoing of his predecessor, Kiyomori. His headquarters, *bakufu*—more administrative offices than palace—were established at his Kamakura home (just south of modern Tokyo).

> ### Cocksure
>
> *When going into battle, it helps to have the gods on your side. By the same token, the gods' earthly representatives, the priests, like to be on the winning side. So it was before the Battle of Dannoura, when Tanzo, head of the local Shinto shrine, asked the gods for a sign as to which banner he should sail under—the white of the Minamoto or the red of the Taira.*
>
> *An oracle suggested white, but Tanzo was not convinced, considering the superior naval experience of the Taira. So, to make sure, he decided to hold a cockfight in front of the shrine—seven red cocks against seven white cocks—and Tanzo would go with the winning colour. The white cocks won by a walkover after the red cocks all ran away, and Tanzo sailed out to the white-bannered Minamoto fleet. The gods—and the cocks—knew what was what.*

But, like all his predecessors, he continued to use the emperor as a tool to confer imperial sanction on *bakufu* decisions. He also relied on court officials at Kyoto to supervise his new government machinery of provincial stewards and constables.

First of the national rulers to take the title of *sei-i tai-shogun* ("barbarian-subduing great general"), Minamoto expanded and consolidated his power by confiscating lands from some of the defeated Taira and redistributing them to his samurai vassals. Other less recalcitrant Taira proprietors kept their lands by transferring allegiance to Minamoto, who sent them one of his men as steward, just to make sure. (Loyalty was an essential element in the ethics of Japanese feudalism, but treachery was a no less frequent feature when dictated by self-interest.)

Yoritomo died in 1199 and the Minamoto feudal structure passed intact to the tutelage of his widow's family, the Hojo, who were content to play regent to a Minamoto figurehead shogun, as the Fujiwara had done with the emperor. The fiction of Japanese imperial power had become infinitely extensible. The emperor at Kyoto, still seconded by a Fujiwara regent at court, legitimized a Minamoto who was himself a military dictator controlled by a Hojo regent. In a country where form and substance were inextricably interrelated, two things counted in politics: symbolic authority and real power. Neither could exist without the other.

In 1274 Japan had to face its first foreign military threat, when the Mongol Emperor Kublai Khan sent an army of 30,000, including Chinese and Korean conscripts, to the north coast of Kyushu. Japan's feudal armies were accustomed to single combat, with an opponent of the same rank. The Mongols' more "democratic" close-formation fighting and superior artillery of crossbows and catapult-bombs quickly won them the early encounters against the samurai swordsmen and archers at Tsushima Island and Hakata Bay. Then providential bad weather forced the Mongols to sail back to Korea.

Seven years later, they returned with a force of 160,000. The Japanese had built a defensive wall along Hakata Bay and confined their armed resistance to a tiny beachhead at Shigashima. Once again, nature stepped in, this time with a typhoon which destroyed half the Mongol fleet and drove away the rest. After this "divine wind" or *kamikaze,* as it was called, Japan enjoyed seven centuries without invasion, reinforcing its self-image as divinely pro-

tected and thus invincible. (In 1945, it was perhaps inevitable that the suicide-squadron of young pilots who made their last-ditch effort to preserve the homeland should take the name of *kamikaze.)*

This fortunate escape from Mongol invasion nonetheless weakened the Kamakura regime. The fighting had brought none of the usual spoils of war that provincial warlords and samurai had come to expect as payment. And the treasury was empty after earthquake, famine and plague had crippled the economy. Buddhist monasteries were using their private armies to support imperial ambitions to bring power back to Kyoto. Worst of all, the Kamakura warriors, resenting the way the Kyoto court referred to them as "Eastern barbarians", sought refinement in a ruinous taste for luxury—extravagant feasts, rich costumes and opulent homes. Kamakura was falling apart.

Creative Turmoil

It was symptomatic of the decline in Kamakura's feudal values that the man who brought about the downfall of the *bakufu* was a turncoat. Originally a vassal of the Minamoto, Takauji Ashikaga successfully masterminded a battle in 1333 to return real governmental power to Kyoto—and then promptly snatched it

33

away by setting himself up as the new shogun.

The subsequent power struggle at first split the country into two imperial courts, and then effective control of Japan was splintered for two centuries among scores of *daimyo* (feudal warlords).

Performing an almost perpetual political tightrope act among the feuding factions, the shogunate of the Ashikaga family nonetheless managed to introduce a triumphant new age of elegance and artistic achievement. When they first arrived, the "Eastern Barbarians" upset the Kyoto nobles by swaggering into town, making off with the prettiest girls at riotous banquets, engaging in bloody street brawls and even setting fire to the imperial palace. But once the

dynastic dispute was resolved in 1392, the Ashikaga shoguns settled down in the Muromachi district of Kyoto that gave this new creative era its name.

The gruff, bluff warriors were quickly seduced by the aristocratic life, bringing to the culture some of their own virile energy, a spirit captured in the simple bold black ink strokes of Muromachi landscape painting in contrast to the delicacy of previous styles. It was no contradiction for a samurai to immerse himself in the intricacies of calligraphy or the tea ceremony. Hunters they remained, but the presentation of, say, a pheasant they had just killed became a moment of aesthetic preoccupation as exquisite as an arrangement of flower petals. Conversely, the poetry, music and dance of the *noh* theatre greatly excited the emotions of the samurai to the point where a performance might end in sword fights and bloodshed.

The warriors' taste for these art forms coincided with a renewed interest in things Chinese, above all in the teachings of Zen Buddhism. Zen had been present in Japan since the 12th century, but began its ascendancy under the Kamakura regime, which found the mystic Chinese philosophy admirably suited to Japanese sensitivity, impressionism and love of form and ritual. The Ashikaga shoguns and their samurai were greatly attracted by an essentially anti-intellectual doctrine that transmitted its truth from master to disciple by practical example rather than the scholastic study of texts. Enlightenment, *satori,* was to be achieved through self-under-

Troubled samurai drew comfort from temple landscape-painting.

standing and self-discipline, combining tranquillity and rugged individualism. After their fierce battles, the warriors recuperated through meditation in the peace of a Zen monastery rock-garden.

The usurper, Takauji Ashikaga, had encouraged the building of Zen Buddhist temples and monasteries, most notably the Tenryuji, as an avowed act of penitence for the bloodshed he had caused in his rise to power. Yoshimitsu (1358–1408), most illustrious of the Ashikaga patrons of the arts, built himself the Golden Pavilion *(Kinkakuji)* as a monastic retreat from which he continued to govern after formally abdicating as shogun.

Meanwhile the Zen monks carved out for themselves powerful and lucrative positions as spiritual (and political) advisers to the shogun and commercial representatives in the resumed trade with China. Japan had sulphur and copper to offer and luxury manufactured items such as picture scrolls, painted folding fans (a Japanese invention) and, above all, tens of thousands of splendidly wrought swords which many Chinese were reluctant to spoil by actually using in battle.

From 1467 to 1568, constant civil war raged up and down the country among some 260 *daimyo* from which a dozen emerged victorious. They had fought with mass armies of infantry, rather than relying on the old cavalry elite. While swords, bows and arrows remained the mainstays of warfare, suddenly matchlocks, muskets and cannons made their appearance. The Europeans had arrived.

In 1543, Portuguese explorers reached Tanegashima Island, off southern Kyushu, followed over the next decade by Portuguese traders and Jesuit missionaries, led by Francis Xavier, who landed at Kagoshima in 1549. Many Kyushu *daimyo* adopted Christianity as a means of winning favour with the Portuguese traders, without necessarily abandoning their Buddhist beliefs or Shinto practices. Converted nine years earlier, *daimyo* Omura founded the port of Nagasaki as a centre for Portuguese trade in 1571. The town was handed over to the Jesuits in 1579. By 1582, Christian converts were estimated at 150,000; by 1615 there were half a million throughout the country. (Through all the vagaries of persecution and war, Nagasaki has remained to this day the major centre of Japanese Christianity.)

Trade with the Portuguese—and Dutch—launched a craze for tobacco, bread, potatoes, clocks, pantaloons and eye-glasses—very often worn as a chic symbol of intellectual superiority rather than as an aid for poor eyesight.

Momoyama Unification

By 1568, when Kyoto was seized from the Ashikaga shogunate, three ruthless generals, Nobunaga, Hideyoshi and Tokugawa, had banded together to crush all remaining opposition. Realizing the importance of Western military technology, Nobunaga mastered the manufacture of gunpowder and made firearms from melted-down temple bells. The triumphant trio were the first to develop the appropriate defences against the new firepower; they replaced the old small castles on high ground protected only by wooden stockades with large central fortresses out of range behind broad moats, surrounded by solid stone ramparts and earthworks strong enough to resist cannon fire.

Cleverest of the three, Nobunaga used another Western weapon, Christianity, against the principal remaining threat to his authority, the Buddhist strongholds surrounding Kyoto. While sending armies out to destroy the monasteries and confiscate their lands, he fostered Christianity to win adepts away from the Buddhist faith.

Nobunaga was assassinated by one of his generals in 1582, and Hideyoshi, who had started out as a simple infantryman, succeeded him. His modest beginnings had given Hideyoshi an insatiable taste for power and wealth. He quickly destroyed the remaining pockets of resistance on Shikoku and overwhelmed the powerful Shimazu clan in Kyushu, while moving his rival Tokugawa away from the capital to the isolated little village of Edo (which grew into modern Tokyo). By 1592 Hideyoshi felt himself strong enough to launch an attack on Korea and China, but his armies were driven back by the massed Chinese troops.

No longer needing the help of the Christians against the Buddhists, Hideyoshi saw in the alien creed a threat to his central authority. Just as the Zen Buddhist monks had been commercial agents for Japan's China trade, so the Jesuits were regarded as front men for Portuguese traders who were distracting provincial *daimyo* from doing business with Hideyoshi. Systematic suppression of Christian activity began in 1587 and ten years later six missionaries and 20 Japanese converts were crucified at Nagasaki.

With the tastes of a *nouveau riche,* Hideyoshi proved a master of the art of conspicuous consumption, contrasting sharply with the restraint shown by the Ashikaga shoguns in their displays of wealth. The gigantic castle he built at Osaka was the biggest Japan had ever seen. It demanded a work force of 30,000 men. This age of extravagance accompanying the country's reunification took its name from Momoyama Palace, one of two fabulously opulent residences in which Hideyoshi covered the walls and pillars—and toilets, too—with gold and silver foil. His most astounding coup was the monstrous Kitano tea ceremony for hundreds of rich and poor followers, who were all obliged to stay to the end—it lasted ten days.

Tokugawa Takes All

Of the cunning, ruthless triumvirate that came out on top at the end of the country's century of civil war, Ieyasu Tokugawa was without doubt the most patient, most prudent—and most treacherous.

When Hideyoshi died in 1598, he hoped to have his five-year-old son continue his "dynasty", initially under the tutelage of five regents. But one of the regents was Tokugawa, who had been biding his time at Edo for 12 years, nurturing dynastic ambitions of his own. He moved quickly to eliminate his strongest rivals, crushing them in 1600 at the great Battle of Sekigahara (near modern Nagoya).

After having the Kyoto court bestow on him the title of shogun in 1603, Ieyasu Tokugawa ensured the future of his dynasty by resigning in favour of his pliant son and continuing to rule from

the wings until his death in 1616. In turn the son abdicated in 1623 and grandson Iemitsu consolidated the Tokugawa position with a long shogunate of 28 years.

For the two and a half centuries of rule from the new capital established at Edo, the Tokugawa organized a tightly controlled coalition of some 260 *daimyo,* skilfully placing key family members and the most

38

trustworthy samurai vassals at strategic points throughout the country.

Himeji Castle epitomized feudal ideal of strength and beauty.

From 1615 to 1635, the Tokugawa shoguns dealt with potential threats of rebellion with a series of military laws governing the lives of the samurai, who then made up about 6 per cent of the population. Their numbers were limited, alliances forbidden and weaponry restricted to swords, bows and arrows, ex-cluding fire-arms. There was even a ban on wheeled vehicles, confining freight-transport to pack horses and human porters.

As an outlet for their aggressive energies in this new era of unaccustomed peace, the samurai were encouraged to pursue martial arts and sumo wrestling.

*A Man's Gotta Do
What a Man's Gotta Do*

One of the most celebrated expressions of the warrior's code of bushido *can be found in the true saga of the 47* ronin *(masterless samurai), a mainstay of popular poetry and* kabuki *theatre.*

In 1700, their original lord, Asano, was taking a lesson in court etiquette in the Tokugawa castle at Edo when a government official insulted him. Contrary to the severe new laws controlling the use of weapons inside the castle, Asano drew his sword and wounded the official. Asano was immediately obliged to commit suicide. His enraged retainers dispersed, vowing revenge. Two years later they banded together again to kill the dastardly government official. In turn, although their act of loyalty was approved, they were obliged to commit suicide, all 47 of them. They became national heroes.

The allegiance of this highly privileged and prestigious group was ensured by cementing their ethical principles in the code of *bushido,* "the way of the warrior": loyalty to one's master, defence of one's status and honour, fulfilment of all obligations.

Some fifty years before Louis XIV hit on the idea of impoverishing his nobles by demanding that they spend all their time and money at the court of Versailles, Tokugawa was making crippling demands on his provincial *daimyo*. Loyalty was enforced by holding their wives and children hostage in Edo. Every other year, the *daimyo* had to attend and provide services at the shogun's court and make large financial contributions to construction of the huge new Edo castle (today the Imperial Palace in Tokyo, even bigger than Hideyoshi's castle at Osaka). All roads into Edo, the most famous being the Tokaido Highway, had checkpoints for guns coming in or wives going out.

One of the most important means of keeping a tight rein on the country was to cut it off from the outside world, to keep Japan Japanese. At first, Ieyasu Tokugawa was eager for foreign trade. He wanted China's silk and encouraged the Dutch and British as good, non-proselytizing Protestants just interested in trade. But he didn't like the Portuguese and Spanish Catholic missionaries, who he felt were undermining traditional Japanese values.

He banned their activities in 1612, and two years later ordered the expulsion of all missionaries and unrepentant Japanese converts. Executions and torture followed. Converts were forced to renounce their faith by trampling crucifixes and effigies of Jesus and Mary. The Catholic Church has counted 3,125 martyrdoms from 1597 (beginning under Hideyoshi) to 1660.

In 1635, the Japanese were forbidden on pain of death to try to go abroad—ship-building was restricted to coastal vessels—and any Japanese already overseas were prevented from returning in case they brought back subversive Christian doctrines. Western books were banned, as well as Chinese books mentioning Christianity. (After the purge of foreigners, only a few Dutch stayed on, strictly confined to Dejima Island in Nagasaki Bay.)

Although this isolation slowed Japan's technological and institutional progress almost to a halt, it did permit a great, distinctive cultural growth with a strong national identity.

The Tokugawa shoguns identified their dynasty with the national ancestral cult of Shinto, glorified by the monumental shrines they built at Nikko. Together with an amalgam of Shinto ritual and official Buddhist conformity, they revived the Confucian ideals of filial piety and obedience to authority to bolster their centralized government.

Commerce thrived, partly in response to the costly demands of the Tokugawa court. Provincial *daimyo* developed monopolies in fisheries, forestry and local agriculture such as sugar cane in Kyushu. Merchants thronged to the large cities growing up around the castles at Edo (population already 1 million in the 18th century), Osaka (400,000), and Nagoya and Kanazawa (both 100,000)—all huge in comparison with European cities of the time. Japan's total population in the 18th century was already about 30 million.

These were the formative years of Japan's great commercial and industrial conglomerates. From a little *sake* brewery on the Ise Peninsula in the 17th century, the Mitsui family moved into pawnbroking, money-lending and dry goods stores in Edo, Kyoto and Osaka to create the gigantic banking, industrial and department store (Mitsukoshi) empire of modern times.

Merchants were low down on the Tokugawas' social totem pole, but very active in creating the urban culture that burgeoned at the end of the 17th century, the so-called Genroku era. It was now that the merchants set the enduring pattern of hard-working, pious family men who, before they went home from work, liked to drink strong alcohol in the company of actresses and prostitutes. (These were the forerunners of the *geisha*—"accomplished person"—with a beauty and refinement that the merchants did not seek in their

41

wives, whom they valued for their child-bearing and good housekeeping.) The Genroku era offered halcyon days for the *noh* theatre, the more popular *kabuki* and grandiose puppet theatre (today's *bunraku*) at Osaka, which was Japan's great cultural capital at a time when Edo had more politicians and soldiers than artists.

The austerity of the Tokugawa regime provided a secure framework for the unique dynamic Japanese mixture of flamboyance with restraint, audacity and discipline, beautifully captured in the colourful woodblock prints of Utamaro, Hiroshige and Hokusai.

In the end it was the very rigidity of the Tokugawas' unshared control of the country that brought about their downfall. They had no flexible response to the ups and downs of the economy. Without access to foreign markets, there was no way to counter the rash of catastrophes —plague, drought, floods and famine—at the end of the 18th century. Uprisings in the towns and countryside began to pose serious threats to the shogun's authority. The Tokugawa reaction was characteristic—a reinforcement of the austere values of the samurai and a clampdown on the merchants' high life. No more gambling, no more barbers, prostitutes were arrested,

men and women were segregated in the public bath-houses—with naked government spies to enforce the (short-lived) new rules.

Crop failures and famine continued in the 1820s and '30s and the shogun took compulsory loans from the merchants to feed the starving peasants. Wages and prices were cut by 20 per cent. The samurai sensed panic in the shogunate and gradually turned their loyalties to the emperor, still the ultimate guarantee of Tokugawa legitimacy, as the enduring symbol of national unity.

The Yankees Are Coming

The feeling began to grow that the only way out of the crisis was to open the country to foreign trade and new ideas. The Tokugawa shoguns, however, sensed that the internal strains might be contained, by sheer brute force if necessary, as long as new pressures were not exerted from outside, with foreigners once again offering disgruntled *daimyo* new sources of income.

Japanese scholars had maintained a minimal acquaintance with Western ideas throughout the Tokugawa era by their discreet contacts with the little Dutch community in Nagasaki Bay. All Western knowledge was classified as *rangaku*, "Dutch learning", with particular respect accorded to the medical sciences. But attitudes remained

Bugaku *court dances – entertainment for emperors.*

distrustful: in 1857 the Institute for the Study of Barbarian Writings *(bansho shirabesho)* was established. Fearful of weakening Japanese values, scholars proclaimed the slogan: "Western science with Eastern ethics".

A few American ships approached Japanese waters in the 1790s on behalf of Dutch traders, but the first real "contact" was in 1837 when the good ship *Morrison* came—unarmed—to Edo Bay to deliver seven Japanese castaways, only to be driven off by cannon fire. Eight years later, a more serious attempt was made when the United States Navy arrived with two warships. They were seeking proper treatment for shipwrecked American sailors, who in the past had been manhandled, but most importantly they wanted Japanese ports of call for fuel and supplies for the Pacific fleet and the general opening of trading and diplomatic relations. They were turned away.

The stubborn American came back again in 1853 with Commodore Matthew Perry bringing for the shogun (whom he mistook for the emperor) a polite but insistent letter from President Millard Fillmore, and a promise to return the next year, with a bigger squadron, for a positive response.

In 1854, Perry duly negotiated the Treaty of Kanagawa (now part of Yokohama—he was not allowed into Edo), opening up two ports, Shimoda on the Izu Peninsula and Hakodate in Hokkaido. A short time later, similar treaties were signed with Britain and Russia. The West had driven in the thin end of its wedge. More and more ports were opened to foreign trade, and the Japanese were obliged to accept low import tariffs.

As the Tokugawa shoguns had feared, this opening of the floodgates of Western culture after such prolonged isolation had a traumatic effect on Japanese society. The Tokugawa had successfully persuaded the

samurai that traditional Japanese values might suffer, and now the samurai felt betrayed, rallying under the slogan *"sonno joi!"* ("Honour the emperor, expel the barbarians!").

Before they could even think of accepting contact with the outside world, national integrity had to be saved under the renewed moral leadership of the emperor. Bands of samurai assassinated British and Dutch representatives. In 1863, the *daimyo* of Choshu in western Honshu fired on foreign ships in the Shimonoseki Straits. In response the United States, British, Dutch and French combined forces to smash the Choshu fortified positions. Britain retaliated for the assassination by practically levelling the town of Kagoshima in southern Kyushu. The local *daimyo* of Satsuma was so impressed that he started buying the British ships that became the foundation of the future Imperial Japanese Navy. Contact with the West might not be so bad after all.

The Meiji Restoration

In January 1868, the Satsuma and Choshu clans, never a real threat to Tokugawa authority as long as they remained rivals, joined forces to overthrow the shogun and restore the authority of the emperor, the 14-year-old Mitsuhito. Edo was renamed Tokyo ("Eastern Capital") and the emperor took over the Tokugawa castle as his palace. His closest court advisers were Fujiwara nobles, whose ancestors had first tasted power back in the 7th century.

But important as the resuscitated imperial authority undoubtedly was, the real power under the Restoration known as Meiji ("Enlightened Rule") was in the hands of a new generation of forward-looking administrators. Dynamic men such as Toshimichi Okubo and Hiro-

Meiji era led inexorably to skyscrapers at the Palace moat.

45

bumi Ito set about abolishing the ancient feudal apparatus in favour of a modern governmental machine based on merit rather than ancestry. They emphasized the need to acquire Western military and industrial skills and technology with which to confront the West itself and eliminate unfair trade tariffs and other unjust aspects of the foreign treaties. (Typically, one of these was a clause exempting foreign residents from the rule of Japanese law, and to change this, the Japanese legal system had to be modernized to gain the foreigners' acceptance. Torture was abandoned as a legally accepted practice, but new attempts to illegalize prostitution and mixed public bathing to please prim Westerners proved ineffective.)

The 260 feudal domains were abolished and reorganized into just 45 prefectures, and the private armies of the *daimyo* were disbanded to form the imperial armed forces, augmented by universal conscription. The feudal privileges of the samurai disappeared—their traditional swords and distinctive topknot hairdo along with their special stipend (commuted into a less lucrative government-bonded pension). The samurai were in a state of shock. A short-lived rebellion in Kyushu epitomized the transformation that had taken place. Takamori Saigo, a hero of the Meiji Restoration, led 40,000 sword-swinging samurai into a suicidal assault on the guns and cannon of the imperial army.

To show just how fast Japan was catching on, two punitive expeditions were launched against Korea and China in the grand

---

Diplomatic Fun and Games

The treaty negotiations at Kanagawa throw a revealing light on the differences between the two cultures. To begin with, the Japanese had good reason to worry about the foreign threat to their integrity. Commodore Perry wrote in his report about wanting to bring to Japan "nobler principles", "better life" and "higher civilization".

For entertainment, the Japanese astounded the Americans with a sumo wrestling contest, while the Americans managed to bewilder their hosts with a negro minstrel show. As gifts, the Americans brought rifles, pistols, swords, telegraph apparatus, Webster's Dictionary, cherry brandy, champagne and 100 gallons of bourbon whisky. But the star attraction was their miniature railway on which the Japanese negotiators had great fun riding up and down. In exchange, the Japanese gave silks, gold lacquerware, porcelain and what Perry described as "a box of obscene paintings of naked men and women, another proof of the lewdness of this exclusive people".

manner of 19th-century gunboat diplomacy.

Economic progress was pursued with the combination of prudence and dynamism that has become Japan's trademark. Agriculture, commerce and traditional manufacturing were expanded to provide a sound economic base for investment in the modern technology of textiles and other industries. Shipbuilding and weapon-manufacture were already under way, railways and telegraph lines quickly followed.

By selling off non-strategic, state-owned industries at low prices during a slump in the 1870s, the government helped create the small elite of *zaibatsu* ("financial cliques") who were behind Japanese imperial expansion in the 20th century. The biggest and best-known of these, Mitsui, Mitsubishi and Sumitomi, disbanded after World War II, are back in operation today.

There was an inevitable reaction to the rapid Westernization. Traditional Japanese theatre, the tea ceremony, *ikebana* flower arrangement, the old martial arts, all came back into favour. In 1890 an important imperial edict on education was issued, promoting Asian (i.e. Chinese and Japanese) values in culture, stressing loyalty to the emperor and general harmony. If the singing in school of military songs such as "Come, foes, come!" or "Though the enemy be tens of thousands strong" seems excessively belligerent today, we should not forget similar jingoistic attitudes in Europe and America at the time.

Going Too Far West

Westernization was more than just a matter of modernizing government and industry. In everyday life, handshaking offered an intriguing alternative to bowing. Suits began replacing kimonos; cutaways, known as moningu *(morning coat), became all the rage at imperial court ceremonies. The word for whatever was "in" was* haikara *("high collar"). The mansions of the* nouveaux riches *suddenly set aside one "Western Room" to be filled with hideous Victorian furniture.*

Baseball arrived soon after the whisky (of which a domestic version was being produced by 1898). But the great craze of the 1880s was ballroom dancing. The government built a special dance hall for ministers to foot it with the wives of Western diplomats, and the prime minister threw a fancy-dress ball at his home, disguising himself as a Venetian noble. This was too much for the still influential conservatives and their uproar killed the dance craze overnight.

It would have been unrealistic to expect Japan to achieve parliamentary democracy in one leap from its centuries-old feudal traditions, but representative government gradually gained acceptance with the evolution of highly combative political parties.

Japan also made a spectacular entrance onto the international stage with military actions against China and Russia. The 1894 Sino-Japanese War for control of Korean markets and the strategic region of southern Manchuria was a triumph for Japan's modernized army over China's larger but less well-organized forces. Even more impressive was Japan's success against the powerful war machine of Tsarist Russia (1904–5), beginning with a surprise night-time attack on the Russian fleet that was repeated some years later at Pearl Harbor. The West made no bones about accepting Japan's occupation of southern Manchuria and the annexation of Korea in 1910. In just 40 years, Japan had established itself as a viable world power according to the criteria of the times.

Triumph and Disaster
The Japan of the 20th century saw a stupendous release of energies that had been pent up for the 250 years of Tokugawa isolation. By 1930, raw material production had tripled the figure of 1900, manufactured goods had increased twelvefold and heavy industry was galloping towards maturity. Not for the last time, the Western powers fretted about the competition, but World War I served only to boost the position of the new Asian rival, with Britain leading the Allies in large orders for munitions. Meanwhile, Japan expanded sales of manufactured goods to Asian and other markets cut off from their usual European suppliers. Merchant shipping doubled in size and increased its income tenfold as the European fleets were destroyed.

Setbacks caused by the European postwar slump were only a spur to redouble efforts in the 1930s by diversifying heavy industry into the machine-making, metallurgical and chemical sectors. The West raised its import tariffs and complained, already, of Japanese "dumping" and cheap oriental (i.e. Japan's colonial) labour. Even the terrible 1923 Tokyo earthquake, which cost billions of dollars, provided another stimulus with the construction boom that followed.

Riding the crest of this economic upsurge were the *zaibatsu* conglomerates, a dozen family-run combines, each involved simultaneously in mining, manufacturing, marketing, shipping and banking. These tightly controlled commercial pyramids were the true heirs to the old feudal structures. The owners cooperated readily with the rising military caste in government when it was to their companies' advantage, but their cosmopolitan education and awareness of foreign market needs made them difficult allies for the narrow-minded militarists.

Japan's progress towards parliamentary democracy was halted in the 1930s by the growing nationalism being imposed on government by the generals and admirals. They proclaimed Japan's mission to bring progress to its backward Asian neighbours in language not so very different from that of the Europeans in Africa or the United States in Latin America. After the Russian Revolution of 1917, the Soviet Union was regarded as a major threat to Japan's security and the army felt it needed Manchuria and whatever other Chinese territory it could control as a buffer against Russian advances. In 1931 the Japanese occupied Manchuria. Then, in 1937, with the popular support of ultra-right-wing groups, the army overrode parliamentary resistance in Tokyo and went to war against the Chinese Nationalists. By 1938, they held Nanking, Hankow and Canton.

Japan's expansionist policies were leading to direct confrontation with the West. Japan hoped that war in Europe would divert the Soviet Union from interference in East Asia, giving Japan a free hand both in China and, through its alliance with Germany, in French Indochina after the defeat of France. The United States responded to the Japanese invasion of Indochina with a trade and fuel embargo, cutting off 90 per cent of Japan's supplies. The result was the attack on the American fleet at Pearl Harbor (December 7, 1941) and total war.

Early successes in the Philippines, Borneo, Malaya, Singapore and the Dutch East Indies enabled Japan to establish the Greater East Asia Co-Prosperity

---

Modern Nonsense
The fierce competition with the West did not diminish the attraction of the Western way of life, especially among the young. On Tokyo's main shopping street, the Ginza, young men and women known as modan boi *and* modan garu, *or* moba *and* moga *for short, dared to walk hand in hand, she smoking a cigarette and he wearing the fashionable horn-rimmed glasses inspired by American movie-comic Harold Lloyd. Conservatives condemned such behaviour as* ero, guro *and* nonsensu *(erotic, grotesque and nonsense).*

Sphere. The "liberation" of these old European colonies created the basis for postwar independence movements proclaiming the Japanese slogan "Asia for the Asians".

The Battle of Midway in June 1942, destroying Japan's four aircraft carriers and soon afterwards its merchant navy and remaining naval air-power, cut Japan off from its empire. In 1944, General Douglas MacArthur was back in the Philippines to direct the island-hopping advance that ended in the massive firebombing of Japan's mostly wood-built cities. In an air raid of 130 B-29's, Tokyo was devastated, losing 100,000 of its inhabitants. But Japan was reluctant to sue for peace because the Allies were demanding unconditional surrender with no provision for maintaining the emperor, the symbolic soul of Japan.

Saying that he did not want to risk further loss of Allied lives, already enormous in the face of fierce Japanese resistance, including the suicidal *kamikaze* air attacks, President Harry Truman finally decided to drop atom bombs on Hiroshima, August 6, and Nagasaki, August 9, 1945.

Meanwhile, on August 8, the Soviet Union entered the Pacific War and the day after marched into Manchuria. Five days later, the Japanese people for the first time heard the voice of Emperor Hirohito, in a radio broadcast, announcing that "the war situation has developed not necessarily to Japan's advantage".

Peace and Prosperity

The U.S. occupation of Japan amazed the populace by its leniency. The 1947 Japanese constitution worked out under American auspices kept the emperor as "the symbol of the state", but "deriving his position from the will of the people with whom resides sovereign power".

War trials were held in 1948 and Hideki Tojo, war-time Prime Minister and Chief of Staff, and six other leaders were hanged. Some 200,000 military officers, government officials and business leaders were removed from office. But to counter what it regarded as the threat of the Soviet Union and China in the Pacific, the United States encouraged the rapid reconstruction of Japan with generous financial aid and relaxation of restrictive laws. The *zaibatsu* conglomerates which had fuelled the Japanese war machine were dismantled but later reorganized in somewhat looser forms and without their negative label. The war-weary Japanese

New Hiroshima rises behind the shell of the "Atomic Dome".

were happy to maintain one restriction: defence expenditure was pegged at less than 1 per cent of the total national budget—a boon for economic expansion.

Parliamentary democracy finally came into its own, though with distinctive Japanese modifications inherent in the traditional interaction of politicians and private companies. It has paid off.

The dynamism of the country's free enterprise system is due in no small way to the government's generous support for private industry through the Finance Ministry and the powerful Ministry of International Trade and Industry. Help takes the form of tax advantages, loan facilities, subsidies, and high import tariffs on competitive foreign goods. (Japan has clearly

For the protection of a new car, an ancient Shinto blessing.

not forgotten its 19th-century trade treaties with the West, when the shoe was on the other foot.)

The prosperity is not without its problems: pollution caused by "dirty" industries; high incidence of stomach ulcers, even suicides, among schoolchildren pressured by over-ambitious parents; and the delicate questions of what to do with nuclear energy and growing rocket technology. But rare economic setbacks such as the 1973 Middle East oil embargo have only stimulated new bursts of energy with the awe-inspiring export strategy and technological innovation of one of the most resilient peoples the world has ever seen.

WHERE TO GO

To help you plan your itinerary, we have divided the country into seven sections—one devoted to Tokyo, where you're most likely to start, to get your bearings and become acquainted with modern Japan; then six regional tours spreading out from the capital to the centres of historic and artistic interest, as well as to sites of natural beauty. We recommend that you split your stay in Tokyo in half. Get over your jet lag and look around for the first few days, then go out into the hinterland, and return to Tokyo for a few more days. Do your shopping at the end; you won't want to drag all that electronic equipment, lacquerware, porcelain or whatever around the countryside.

Getting Around

Visiting Japan is an adventure, but not an impossible adventure. A few simple rules of thumb can help Westerners overcome the culture shock of confronting the country's sheer "foreignness". The shock may come because the Western-style urban landscape of your first port of call—Tokyo —will seem at first deceptively familiar. This initial familiarity is reinforced by Japan's internationally known advanced technology, efficient public transport, and its people hurrying about, not in exotic costume, but in business suits, dresses or blue jeans "like you and me".

Then it begins to dawn on you that signs are written in Japanese and that fewer people speak English than you might have been led to expect in such a modern country. But before a sense of chilly panic sets in, take a deep breath and another look. Most of the street signs, subway stops, hotel and shop names, in fact practically all the places foreign visitors are likely to need when getting their first bearings, are spelled out in Roman lettering, too. And enough people do speak the few words of English that you'll need when getting from one place to another, buying what you want or eating what you fancy.

Above all, you're in a country where courtesy seems almost innate. It's part of the people's own survival kit for co-existing in such a densely populated country. Don't be surprised, for instance, if the person of whom you ask the way abandons what he is doing to guide you to the place you're looking for. On the other hand, don't expect people to be forever apologizing for bumping into you on the crowded streets—they'd never have time for anything else.

In the Berlitz-Info section at the back of the book, we give

detailed practical guidance on the day-to-day needs of your trip. Here, however, are a few general words of advice on how to "handle" Japan:

Unless you already speak good Japanese, stick to English. It may be fun to exchange a few words or phrases in Japanese— a polite *arigatō* ("thank you"), *kon nichi wa* ("how are you?"), or, of course, *sayonara* ("good-bye")—but if you try to get into a fully fledged conversation, you'll open up the Japanese floodgates and be unable to get back to the dry land of simple communication. Speak slowly and clearly, without unduly raising your voice. The phrases in the Berlitz-Info section at the back of the book and in the Berlitz phrase book, *Japanese for Travellers,* will help you in situations where you need to speak some Japanese.

Carry a pocket-size notebook. However much improvisation you usually like on holiday, you'll find a certain amount of planning absolutely necessary in Japan. Each morning, before you set out from your hotel, write down in clear Roman capital letters, the places you want to go to. With the aid of street maps, check the closest subway station or bus stop and the line you take to get there. Hotel re-

Travelling in the Tokyo subway demands a certain stoicism.

ceptionists will help you with this and perhaps add the appropriate Japanese characters. Now you have something to show policemen or passers-by. Since the house-numbering of Japanese addresses follows what is, for

Westerners, indecipherable logic, you can also use your notebook to draw little diagrams locating your exact destination in relation to the nearest well-known building. The Japanese are extremely good at this and you end up with a nice bonus of hand-drawn souvenir maps! You'll also need to jot down the Japanese words for things you want to buy—again hotel staff will gladly add the Japanese characters for you to show the sales people.

Use the Japan National Tourist Organization (JNTO). In Tokyo and Kyoto they have English-language Tourist Information Centres (TIC)—see p. 239. Anywhere else, there's a marvellous "Travel-Phone" service that connects you to the English-speaking JNTO network (see p. 241). In major cities, the TIC provides English-speaking guides, usually university students working as unpaid volunteers.

Use public transport. Japan's public transport system is one of the best in the world. Ever since the Americans brought them their first miniature railway in 1854, the Japanese have had a non-stop, full-speed-ahead love affair with their trains, which are clean, efficient and fast (the famous *shinkansen* "bullet" linking the major cities on Honshu island zips along at 130 miles [210 km.] per hour). Ste-

wardesses serve packed lunch, with a hot towel that seems at first a delightful oriental luxury and then becomes a necessity you feel *must* be introduced back home. Buses need a little more study but, with that all-important notebook in which to work out the itinerary beforehand, they are also well worth the effort as a way of seeing neighbourhoods you might otherwise miss. (Taxis should be kept for late-night trips and emergencies, as they are rather expensive and by no means faster in the congested cities.) The most important point is that first-time visitors without a command of the Japanese language should avoid renting a car. It will only cause headaches; away from the city centres, road signs make no language concessions to foreign travellers. For relatively short distances in towns like Kyoto or Nara with lots of temples, monasteries and castles, a rented bicycle can be fun, if you're good at studying maps. (For fuller public transport details, see p. 240.)

Visit the Japanese in their own homes. Yes, this is possible, even if you don't know a soul in Japan, through the JNTO's "Home Visit Programme". As curious about meeting foreigners as you might be to meet them, Japanese families in almost every major city have volunteered to receive foreign visitors in their homes (see p. 233). The hospitality is entirely free of charge, but it's the Japanese custom when visiting somebody's home to take a small gift. This could be a souvenir from your home town; or, if you have nothing suitable, you can go into a good shop and ask for *temiyage*. You will be handed a parcel beautifully wrapped in a cloth *(furoshiki)*. Do not be insulted if your gift is accepted with seeming disdain and not even opened in your presence—your host does not want to embarrass you. When you leave you will probably be handed back your *furoshiki*, which will now contain a small present for you.

Be ready to take your shoes off when going indoors. This custom, rooted in the Japanese religiously inspired aversion to dirt and the quite understandable belief that shoes bear the dirt of the streets, applies to private homes, Japanese-style hotels, restaurants and, above all, temples, but also wherever you see *tatami* floors. So slip-on shoes without laces are the most convenient. You can leave them quite safely at the entrance, as no harm will come to them in this scrupulously honest country. Indoors, you'll find clogs available for tiled floors such as bathrooms and toilets or slippers for carpeted areas.

There are Western-style hotels in every major town you're likely to visit, but don't be afraid to try at least once the experience of a Japanese inn. (The JNTO can make reservations for you at places participating in its new Welcome Inn Service, see p. 220). There are various kinds. The *minshuku* is an inexpensive family-style hostelry—very friendly—where you eat at a table with other guests and have a mattress-bed on the *tatami* floor. The *ryokan* is a grander, more expensive inn where you're treated like a shogun, received by your own personal maid with a welcome tea and sweets in a beautifully designed room, usually overlooking a lovely garden. A piping hot bath, *ofuro*, is prepared and then a royal dinner is served right there in your room. The long *yukata* cotton kimono is provided in every Japanese hotel for your use (but not to take away, though you can buy it). If you splash out on only one thing in Japan, we recommend the *ryokan*. Choose an appropriate place to do it, like imperial Kyoto, since the aesthetics are essential enjoying the experience.

Learn to take the rain in your stride. Yes, it does rain a little more frequently in Japan than you might be used to, but not really enough to spoil your visit. Take a leaf out of the Japanese book:

they always carry with them a little collapsible umbrella, or else pick up a plastic throwaway provided by most hotels and many restaurants. And they welcome the rain as an embellishment of their beloved landscape. The rock gardens of Kyoto take on a whole new mystery in the rain.

One more word before you set out on your sightseeing: don't expect every monument you see to be an original. Given the constant ravages of earthquake, fire and war in a civilization essentially built of wood, the Japanese have learned to attach more importance to the enduring general

Rain brings its own charms, here at Nikko's Yomeimon Gate.

spirit behind the creation, transferred from the original to subsequent copies, than to the art work's individual creativity inherent, for the West, in the original. But don't worry: in Nara, Kyoto and Nikko, spared at least the bombs of World War II, you'll find plenty of major art works with the proper patina of age necessary for a Westerner's seal of approval.

TOKYO

Originally known as Edo ("Estuary"), Tokyo was only a sleepy little village surrounded by marshland on the broad Kanto plain until the end of the 16th century, when Ieyasu Tokugawa moved here to run his fiefdom. After he took over as shogun in 1603 and made Edo his headquarters, the town had to expand fast to house Tokugawa's 80,000 retainers and their families. By the census of 1787 the population had shot up to 1,368,000. During the Tokugawas' time, Edo had a strictly political atmosphere, playing the role of a Washington D.C., while Osaka was the fashionable and arts-conscious "New York". But by 1868, when the Meiji Restoration moved the imperial court to Edo, changing its name to Tokyo ("Eastern Capital"), the cultural focus had already moved to the centre of political power.

In the 20th century, Tokyo has twice suffered almost total destruction: the earthquake of 1923 and subsequent fire which razed nearly all vestiges of old Edo—and killed 140,000 people—and the 1945 firebomb air raids at the end of World War II, which ravaged the still largely wood-built city. Today, with an uncompromising silhouette of skyscrapers capped by an occasional high-fenced rooftop golf driving-range on which amateurs practise their swing, Tokyo very matter-of-factly accepts its function as urban centre of Japan's modernity, leaving to Kyoto the role of faithful repository of the country's ancient traditions and culture.

And so, as you ride the bus or hotel limousine into town from Narita Airport, don't expect a city that combines its business and politics with classical monuments and palaces. Tokyo is a concentration of initially disturbing but gradually exciting vibration, movement and colour—and people, people, people. This astounding congestion goes on all day long, miraculously moving around, functioning with an efficiency that still has the rest of the world breathless with admiration. It functions, not as a huge, soulless automaton, but as an intensely human organism divided into a series of neighbourhoods, even villages, each with its own personality. To get a feel for Tokyo, you must go beyond the sightseeing landmarks to explore these neighbourhoods.

Shinjuku

Your first day in Tokyo will be like one of those scalding hot Japanese baths. The initial shock is considerable, but it won't kill you. In fact, you'll find it exhilarating. Above all, don't just dip one toe in, immerse yourself up to the neck: start at Shinjuku.

Actually north-west of the city's downtown area, this neighbourhood is total Tokyo: elegant, prosperous business quarter to the west, exuberant high and low life to the east, and underground a whole other teeming city of shops, boutiques, cafés and *sushi* bars. An instant lesson in population density.

Make your way there by train on the Marunouchi subway line and get off at one of the great wonders of the 20th century: **Shinjuku Station**, biggest in Japan. Difficult as it is to measure such things, it's impossible to imagine there's anywhere busier in the world. Just once—not many foreigners can handle it twice—try to get there on a weekday before 8.30 a.m. You missed the building of Egypt's Pyramids, but as a consolation, you get to see the people of Tokyo going to work. Official statistics claim that 3,600,000 people pass through Shinjuku Station on a working day. Most of them seem to be there before 8.30 a.m. The by now world-famous "people-pushers" perform incredible feats of strength on the platforms squeezing "just one more" on the train. Occasionally, they overdo it and have to become people-pullers to get some off for the doors to close. Inside, the passengers close their eyes, not, as you might think, to fall asleep, but just to shut out the surrounding surfeit of humanity. It works. Nobody panics. Everybody gets on and off at the right station.

West of the railway station is a cluster of a dozen gleaming concrete, steel and glass office blocks, some of them soaring up to 60 storeys over ground that is said to be, per square metre, the world's most costly property. Take your first bird's-eye view of the city with a ride up to the observation deck on the 51st floor of the **Sumitomo Building**, offices of one of the original mammoth *zaibatsu* conglomerates that helped build the old Japanese empire (see p. 48). (If the weather is clear, you may glimpse Mt. Fuji to the southwest—don't pass up the photo opportunity, because on your trip out there, the sacred peak may be shrouded in mist.)

Away from the rather rarefied atmosphere of the office skyscrapers, the boisterous side of Shinjuku begins to show. The neighbourhood attracts people from every layer of society—in addition to the businessmen, you'll find artists, political activists, students, ladies of the night (and day) and visitors from Tokyo's rustic hinterland, as wide-eyed with wonder as you may be.

Around **Higashi-guchi** east of Shinjuku Station, in the bustling area of camera discount shops, people stop to watch the giant open-air television screen covering the whole upper façade of the Studio Alta building. The crowds attract the attentions of neo-fascist orators hectoring passers-by with ear-blasting megaphones from atop formidable black-painted trucks bearing the flag of the old Japanese Imperial Army.

Just north of this shopping district behind Meiji-Dori Avenue, striking a more cheerful and downright lurid note, is the colourful entertainment quarter of **Kabuki-cho**. Cinemas, student coffee-shops and *sushi* bars share the neighbourhood with strip-saloons, snug little nightclubs, halls offering female sumo wrestling, cafés proposing "coffee and peeping", love-hotels for the lovelorn-in-the-afternoon, and public baths known as *sōputando*, "soap land". The range of exotic activities is endless, and the best-paying customers are unabashed senior executives from those office skyscrapers on the "right" side of the railway tracks. Come back after dark and watch these kings of capitalism at play.

Beneath it all is the **Subnade** (*sub*terranean prome*nade*) of shops, cafés and bars, about 150 at last count, and expanding. Rain or cold drives the business underground and sun brings it back up—except weekends, when everybody's everywhere, up and down.

To "cool off" from this, your

61

first bath in metropolitan Japan, take a rest in the lovely **Shinjuku Gyoen National Garden,** southeast of the skyscrapers and a popular place for viewing the cherry blossoms, if you're there in April, or the chrysanthemum displays in November.

Marunouchi

This is the geographical centre of Tokyo, graceful, spacious, remarkably less crowded than the rest of the city. Here you'll see the imposing modern towers that house the headquarters of the country's major banking and industrial institutions in prestigious proximity to the **Imperial Palace**.

For 265 years the stronghold of the Tokugawa shoguns before being handed over to the imperial family in 1868, the palace was almost totally destroyed by firebombs in 1945. Reconstruction was completed in 1968—in non-flammable ferroconcrete— in traditional Japanese style, but the gable-roofed silhouette you see today is only a fraction of the size of the original gigantic structure. Perhaps the most impressive features of the palace, epitomizing the remote and for the most part inaccessible position of the emperor himself, are the

Picnickers come out to enjoy the cherry blossom in Shinjuku Gyoen.

Memories on Kudan Hill

*History buffs fascinated by the modern evolution of Japanese military tradition may like to make a side trip to the **Yasukuni Shrine** up on Kudan Hill at the north-west corner of the Imperial Palace ramparts (Kudanshita subway station).*

This Shinto sanctuary is approached through two towering torii gates, one of bronze, one of granite. In the outer precincts, a huge bronze statue of Masujiro Omura (1824-1869), first war minister after the Meiji Restoration, was dedicated in 1896 to "the divine spirits of those who gave their lives in defence of the Empire of Japan". According to the dedication, the shrine of Yasukuni— "Peaceful Country"—contains the names of 2,500,000 who died in military service up to 1945. Pacifists protest the nationalistic spirit it inspires among old war veterans whom you can see on regular pilgrimages to pay homage and be photographed in front of the shrine with survivors of their old combat units.

The cherry blossoms on Kudan Hill are especially spectacular in early spring, when old soldiers recall the celebrated oath they once made with now fallen comrades: "Let us meet again beneath the cherry trees of Kudan".

Spring and autumn festivals are held at the shrine every year in April and October.

great moat and massive sloping black volcanic stone ramparts enclosing the Imperial Gardens. The impact of what would otherwise be a most forbidding fortress is nicely softened by the creeping ivy and overhanging trees at the top of the ramparts— and the red-beaked black swans and goldfish in the moat.

The emperor still resides in the palace, so the general public is only admitted to the inner grounds two days in the year— January 2 for the important New Year's holiday and December 23 for the emperor's birthday—but on these occasions you'd find it hard to compete with the thousands of Japanese visitors who cram in. At other times private arrangements can be made in advance by limited foreign groups— armed with passports—through the Imperial Household Agency.

But the outer palace grounds do offer a more accessible and very welcome haven from the city bustle; the **Imperial Palace East Garden** is open to the public every day except Monday and Friday. (On Sunday, bicycles are available free of charge.) From Otemachi subway station, you enter the gardens at the Otemon Gate. Wander through a maze of hedgerows of white and shocking

Tokyo's gleaming Marunouchi district is where the money is.

pink azaleas or around ponds and little waterfalls edged by pines, plum trees, canary palms and soft green *cryptomeria japonica*. In the time-honoured manner of laying out Japanese gardens, particular attention is given to incorporating distant vistas (perhaps snowcapped mountains or dark forests) for the harmony of the overall effect, a technique known as "borrowed landscape". In this case, a perhaps unintentional twist is given to the centuries-old art when, beyond the tranquil greenery, over the tree tops, you catch a startling glimpse of the skyscrapers of modern Tokyo.

On your way back to Otemachi Station, stop on Eitai-dori Avenue to admire the graceful wedge-shaped polished amberstone building of the **Industrial Bank of Japan**. Built by Murano Togo in 1974, this is truly a masterpiece of modern form amid the otherwise unremarkable cigar-box office blocks.

The Ginza

Tokyo's smartest and doubtless best-known district is named after a silver mint originally located here, though prices today in the department stores and high-class restaurants are

The bright lights of Akihabara beckon the hesitant customer.

pure gold—kept that way by Japanese executives' tax-deductible expense accounts. But the shops nonetheless exert their fascination, and it's worthwhile at least window-shopping here before making for the discount paradise of Akihabara's electronics stores (see p. 201).

In any case, department stores such as Mitsukoshi or Matsuya, in addition to first-class exhibitions of prints and paintings in their art galleries, offer to Western eyes veritable works of art in their basement food-department displays. (The basement is also a good place for cheaper snacks than you'll find in the street-level restaurants). But it's in the side streets off the main Ginza thoroughfare that you'll find the most fascinating avant-garde art galleries, little bars, cafés and boutiques. The whole constitutes one of the best people-watching spots in the country—enhanced by what is in the evening a positively national institution: a walk around the Ginza or *gin-bura* ("silver stroll"). Join in.

At the southern edge of the Ginza district is the enormous **Tsukiji Central Wholesale Market**—with plenty of retail stalls, too. On sale are meat, fruit and vegetables, but above all the freshest of fresh fish right on the waterfront of Tokyo Bay. Get there very early for a good and amazingly cheap Japanese

breakfast that will do for lunch as well, and then watch no-nonsense housewives and haughty *haute cuisine* chefs vying for the best products with that bewitching mixture of unfailing courtesy and relentless dedication to the task in hand. Or else take a picnic down to the lovely **Hama Detached Palace Garden**, a masterpiece of Edo-period landscaping incorporating a view of the Sumida Estuary and Tokyo Bay.

Harajuku

Japan's most venerable imperial traditions and the modern celebration of the youth culture of rock 'n roll and motorbikes live happily side by side in Harajuku (south of Shinjuku).

Either Meiji-Jingu-mae Station on the Chiyoda subway line or Harajuku Station on the Yamanote circular line of the Japanese National Railways (JNR) takes you to Yoyogi Park and the **Meiji Shrine**. Rebuilt in 1958 after its destruction in World War II, the shrine was dedicated in 1920 to Meiji and his wife Shoken after their deaths in the days when the emperor was still regarded as a deity.

You pass through a grand cypress-wood *torii* gate, ceremonial entrance to all Shinto shrines, up

Jap-punk and grimace-kings, all eccentrics flock to Harajuku.

a long, tree-shaded avenue to another, larger *torii* leading directly to the shrine itself. The structure's impressive modern refinement of classical Shinto architecture is an apt symbol of the Meiji Restoration, which prepared Japan for the modern age while renewing the ancient imperial traditions. In early May and November, the Emperor Meiji is commemorated with festivals of *bugaku* court music and dancing from the golden Heian era of the 12th century. A lovely Iris Garden just south-west of the shrine is at its best in late June and early July.

The modern age starts south of the Meiji Shrine Inner Garden in **Yoyogi Park**. If you're interested in how they make those samurai soap operas that you may have seen on Japanese televi-

sion at the hotel, you must visit the **NHK Broadcasting Station**. Your hotel or the TIC will tell you how to take the Ken-Ga-Ku tour of the backlots and soundstages that recreate the great ages of Japanese history.

But the park is above all a sports complex, created for the 1964 Olympics, where you can see Kenzo Tange's dramatically curving, seashell-shaped **Olympic Stadium**, with a roof that has neither beams nor columns to block the spectators' view.

East of the park is a neighbourhood forming the teenage playground that most Tokyoites think of when you say Harajuku, in the alleyways around Meiji-dori and Omote-sando avenues. Here among the novelty stalls and flea market where they get their gear, bands of *takenokozuku*—literally "bamboo-shoots", oriental cousins of American teenyboppers—and occasional *bosozoku*, somewhat older, leather-jacketed motorbikers, gather at the weekend to dance to the latest music amplified on the latest Japanese equipment. Deadly earnest, boys and girls dance, often completely separate, strangely stylized and unhysterical; Harajuku's assimilation of American culture offers a distant echo of the years when the GIs of the United States Army Occupation Forces lived here in what they called Washington Heights.

Asakusa

If the Ginza is the major focus for the foreign tourists and the Tokyo bourgeoisie and Harajuku for the switched-on young, then Asakusa (north-east of the downtown area) remains the popular favourite for Japanese visitors coming in from the provinces. Without a doubt, it's the most cheerful, happy-go-lucky neighbourhood in the city, perhaps the one place that retains something of the atmosphere of the days when Tokyo was Edo.

Characteristic of the uninhibited attitude that the Japanese have always entertained towards their religion, Asakusa is not only the home of the city's major Buddhist temple, next to an important Shinto shrine, but also the jolliest of old-fashioned entertainment districts. Here the warlords and samurai under the Tokugawa shogunate paid visits to the geisha girls, and Tokyo saw its first cinema show, at the Denki-Kan ("Electricity Pavilion") in 1903, only eight years after the Lumière brothers' historic world première in Paris. Religion and pleasure were and still are very happily combined.

The liveliest moment to come here (Asakusa Station on the Ginza subway line) is late afternoon. Through the great Kaminarimon Gate, you enter the long **Nakamise** arcade leading to the temple and shrine, in fact a

70

permanent street market with the boisterous atmosphere of a country fair. A five-storey pagoda (copy of the Daigoji in Kyoto) towers over food stands offering barbecued chicken, corn on the cob, *sushi* rice balls or fried *tempura* vegetables and fish, which you can wash down with lemonade in old-fashioned bottles with glass marbles lodged inside the neck. Clowns and acrobats prance around souvenir stalls touting statues of the Buddha, portable Shinto shrines for ancestral ashes—and live turtles and baby crabs as lucky mascots.

Wise old ladies astound you with fortunes told from chopsticks, while old men confound each other over open-air games of *go* or chess.

Protected by the statues of four ferocious guardians of the deities, the delightfully garish Sensoji is also popularly known as the **Asakusa Kannon Temple**, dedicated to the Kannon or female embodiment of the Buddha's spirit of mercy and thus simplified in the popular consciousness as a Goddess of Mercy. Recently rebuilt in ferro-concrete after being twice de-

---

Mickey Mouse in Tokyo

*One of the city's most popular tourist attractions is **Tokyo Disneyland** (the first to be built outside the United States), but then you must remember that most tourists in Tokyo are Japanese. This mammoth amusement park, built on the model of the theme parks in California and Florida, follows the now classical pattern of scaled-down introductions to the American way of life and the American way of seeing the world, past and present, along with Walt Disney-style adventure—boat rides through the "jungle", pirate galleons, old-fashioned silent-movie cinemas and space-rockets.*

The park is divided into four "theme" areas—Adventureland, Westernland, Fantasyland and To-

morrowland. One of the major specifically Japanese contributions is in the Tomorrowland area, an attraction called "Meet the World". This shows the history of Japan's friendlier contacts with the outside world, such as with the Portuguese, the Chinese and the Americans, using all the most modern electronic equipment available in Japan for the audio-visual effects to recapture the people and places of the past.

You should make advance reservations at major Tokyo travel agencies or through Japan Air Lines. Best way to the park—on the eastern outskirts of the city—is by the special Tokyo Disneyland shuttle leaving every ten minutes from downtown Tokyo Station's Yaesu north entrance.

stroyed by earthquake and war in the 20th century, the temple originally dates back to the 7th century when three fishermen are said to have found in their nets a tiny gold statue of the Kannon and set it up near this site in a sanctuary of reeds.

In 1651, at a time when the Tokugawa shoguns were reinforcing Buddhism as a national religion, a major temple was founded here by the Tendai sect, which proposed an amalgam of the various competing Buddhist doctrines. As the most important temple in the capital, the Asakusa Kannon became the focus of a pilgrimage reinforcing national unity. The shoguns' political imperatives are long forgotten, but Asakusa remains a popular national pilgrimage, in no small part because it's also a lot of fun.

West of the temple grounds, around Shibasakicho Street, is the entertainment district proper, **Rokku.** For the children, there's an old-style amusement park, valiantly resisting the electronic game-halls and *pachinko* parlours. But the main attraction is the plethora of theatres, music halls such as the Roxy and the gigantic Shochiku All-Girl Opera House. Geisha houses continue the venerable tradition, as well as striptease saloons, *sōputando* baths and love hotels. Something for every member of the family.

Ueno

North of the city centre, Ueno was the site of the Tokugawa shogunate's last stand against the Imperial Army in 1868 and subsequently became the first city park of Tokyo's more democratic era. Swiss architect Le Corbusier participated in the planning of today's park, popular with Tokyo residents for picnics, baseball and museum-hopping.

If you take the Ginza subway line to Ueno Station, you can enter the park at the southern corner by the massive statue of Takamori Saigo, national hero both as commander-in-chief of the Imperial Army against the Tokugawas and later rebel against the imperial forces themselves (see p. 46).

Of the park's half dozen museums, the most important—in fact, the largest in the country—is the **Tokyo National Museum** (at the northern end of the park), devoted to Japanese art and archaeology dating back to the earliest prehistoric Jomon and Yayoi periods. Outstanding among the later exhibits are Buddhist sculpture and painting of the 10th- and 11th-century Heian era, illustrated narrative scrolls from the 13th-century Kamakura period, paintings by the

At Meiji Shrine, people clap hands to attract gods' attention.

great Muromachi artist, Sesshu, and the celebrated prints of the Edo masters Hiroshige, Utamaro and Hokusai. Look, too, for excellent displays of lacquerware, *noh* theatre costumes and masks, samurai armour and weapons.

South-west of the National Museum is the **Tokyo Metropolitan Fine Art Gallery**, which specializes in Japanese art of the 20th century. Look out for the excellent temporary shows for an idea of the great visual creativity of the current generation.

If you want to take a break from things Japanese, there's the **National Museum of Western Art**, designed by Le Corbusier, on the east side of the park. The collection includes works by Tintoretto, El Greco, Goya, Rubens, most of the French Impressionists. Modern masters are represented notably by Picasso, Max Ernst and Jackson Pollock.

And if the children want a break from human beings, take them to the compact little **Ueno Zoological Garden** (on the park's west side).

More Museums

Here are a few more from among the dozens of Tokyo museums, many of them privately owned by big companies:

Idemitsu Art Gallery (Yurakucho subway station). A private collection with a beautiful modern display of ancient Chinese bronzes, Chinese Buddhist sculpture from the 5th to the 7th centuries, and Japanese paintings and screens from the 15th to 17th centuries.

Bridgestone Museum (Kyobashi subway station). Owned by a Japanese rubber magnate named Ishibashi, which translates as Bridgestone. Some good French Impressionists (Manet, Monet, Cézanne) plus Picasso. Save this for your last day in Japan, if possible, as a mental preparation for the trip home.

Sword Museum (Sangubashi Station on Odakyu line from Shinjuku). Nice introduction to the noble and lethal history of Japanese swords, the closest that weapons ever came to being great works of art.

Japan Folk Arts Museum—Mingeikan (Komaba Todai-mae Station on the Inokashita Line from Shibuya). Excellent examples of ceramics, lacquerware, woodcraft and textiles. It gives a particularly good insight into Japanese furniture that you may not get to see in a private home.

Goto Art Museum (Kaminoge Station on the Den-en-Toshi line). Fine private collection of 13th- and 14th-century (Heian and Kamakura) Japanese painting, including some rare illustrated scrolls, *emakimono*, of scenes from Japan's supreme literary masterpiece, *Genji Monogatari* (*Tale of the Genji*).

KANTO

The once marshy plain of Kanto is Tokyo's hinterland. This is where the feudal warlords set up their military bases and administrative headquarters as alternative *de facto* political capitals to what they regarded as the effete and decadent imperial court of Kyoto. Their tough-minded pragmatism survives today not only in Tokyo but also in the dynamic industrial zone that has burgeoned around it in such towns as Kawasaki and the flourishing port of Yokohama. The monuments to the warlords' political domination remain in the old military headquarters of Kamakura and the Tokugawa shoguns' own extravagant mausoleums at the Nikko National Park. And reigning supreme at the south-west edge of the plain, sublime spiritual comment on the vanity of all such human endeavour, is sacred Mt. Fuji.

(Except for Mt. Fuji, each of the sightseeing destinations of the Kanto region can make a convenient day trip if you want to keep Tokyo as your base.)

Nikko

Like the Pharaohs of ancient Egypt, the Tokugawa shoguns provided for their own glorification by having themselves enshrined as deities in grandiose mausoleums—so grandiose that the building conveniently impov-

Tokugawa's tomb at Nikko stands in a magnificent forest setting.

erished the vassal warlords who had to foot the bill. The place they chose was Nikko, about 90 miles (150 km.) north of the capital in a magnificent hilly site above the rushing Daiya River, to the east of Lake Chuzenji. The hills are covered by a beautiful cedar forest—13,000 splendid trees left from the 40,000 painstakingly planted by Masatsuna Matsudaira, a lord who is said to have found this cheaper than contributing to the construction of the shrines. The result is a superb national park, one of the best loved in all Japan, a natural setting that many feel is more majestic than the Tokugawa shoguns could possibly have imagined—or deserved.

The train journey from Tokyo

takes about two hours (JNR from Tokyo's Ueno Station or private Tobu-Nikko line from Asakusa Station). This makes a good day trip if you want just to see the monuments and something of the surrounding countryside. On the other hand, if you'd like to explore the park a little further—the lake, the waterfalls and the forest—as well as the great monuments, it is best to make an overnight stay.

The route you take has an exhilarating orchestrated quality to it, blending natural and man-made effects with impressive harmony. The dramatic overture, at the northern edge of town, is **Shinkyo Sacred Bridge**, a 92-foot (28-m.) span across the Daiya River. The gracefully curving vermilion-lacquered bridge on sturdy *torii*-shaped supports marks the spot where the 8th-century Buddhist priest Shodo is said to have crossed the torrential stream on the backs of two huge serpents on his way to found Chuzenji Temple. Another tale, picked up by English writer Rudyard Kipling, suggests that the bridge's curve reproduces the arc of blood that spurted across the river when a warlord cut a beggar's head off with his sword. The warlord, who had been admiring the dark beauty of the rugged landscape, found the red enhanced it with just the right touch of colour.

Omotesando, a gently sloping path to the shrines, begins north of the river. The Nikko sanctuary, promoting the ancestral worship of the Tokugawa dynasty, represents the shoguns' effort to appropriate at least a share in the national Shinto cult that had previously been the preserve of the imperial family. So, manifestations of Buddhism in the area are relatively muted, one of them being the **Rinnoji Temple** of the eclectic Tendai Buddhist sect, to the right of Omotesando. It was originally presided over by an imperial abbot through whom the Tokugawa family obtained the emperor's spiritual blessing— notice the imperial chrysanthemum crest on a gilded reliquary in the Spirit Hall.

The temple's principal hall is the **Sambutsudo**, housing three huge gilt wooden Buddha statues (the manifestations of the Buddha taking many forms). The central figure is the Amida Nyorai, through whom the Tendai priests popularized Buddhism by making nirvana accessible to the common man merely by his repeating a simple invocation to Amida rather than the elaborate spiritual exercises and meditation of the traditional cult. On the right is the 1,000-handed Kannon, actually with 40 hands but each able to fulfil 25 of the faithfuls' wishes. To the left is the Bato Kannon, with the figure of a horse's head in the forehead, symbol of the Buddha's protection of animals. The **Shoyoen Garden** is a characteristic "strolling" (as opposed to contemplative) garden of the Tokugawa Edo period, a beautiful blend of nature and artifice.

Omotesando, like all approaches to popular shrines, is lined with souvenir stalls, fortune tellers using birds to bear your secret wishes to the gods, and food and drink vendors (excellent fresh fruit juices).

Toshogu is the great, the immense shrine housing the spirit and tomb (in two separate places) of Ieyasu Tokugawa, founder of the dynasty that governed Japan for over 250 years (see p. 38). Following his detailed instructions, the mausoleum was begun in 1634 (18 years after his death) by his grandson Iemitsu. It took 15,000 workers, most of them brought in from Nara and Kyoto, home of the country's most skilled carpenters and artisans. The meticulous book-keeping noted that 2,489,000 sheets of gold leaf were used to decorate the sculptures and buildings—enough to gild two football fields.

It all begins very modestly with a stairway-entrance of ten broad stone steps beyond which the lower classes in the old days were not allowed to go. Beyond the tall granite *torii*, to the left, is the 115-foot (35-m.) Five-Storey Pagoda, bearing the three-petal hollyhock crest of the Tokugawa. Nearby are booths for tickets to enter the main shrine.

A first note of ambitious ornament is struck when the central stone path leads you to the elaborately carved **Omotemon Gate**, guarded by two stone Deva Kings grimacing fiercely to frighten off evil spirits—and impressionable children. The next courtyard contains sacred storehouses. If the carved elephants look a little strange, it's because they're based on the fanciful drawings of 17th-century artist Tanyu Kano, who had never seen an elephant and had to rely on written descriptions. To the left is the stable of the shrine's sacred white horse, protected by sculptures of the three wise monkeys who "hear no evil, speak no evil, see no evil" and are quite clearly astounded by the evil they have to ignore. The stone and iron lanterns dotted around the courtyard were donated as marks of respect by *daimyo* vassals grateful for the opportunity to finance the great shrine.

Equally grateful—for being granted exclusive trading rights after all other foreigners had

Yomeimon Gate's extravagant ornamentation is Nikko's centrepiece.

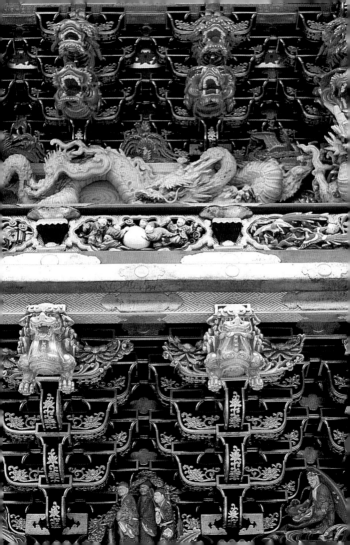

been expelled from Japan—the Dutch government donated the bronze lantern and candelabra you can see near the belfry and drum tower to the right and left as you approach the **Yomeimon Gate**. This two-storey "Gate of Sunlight" 37 feet (11.3 m.) high and built of Caucasian elm, is the extravagant masterpiece of Nikko. No Roman or Napoleonic arch was ever more triumphal. Its Baroque profusion of grinning, grimacing lions, dragons, tigers, long-necked horses, phoenixes, pheasants, ducks, sweet little children and ancient wise men surrounded by painted clouds, pines, plum-trees and flowers, is the ultimate flourish of Japan's opulent Momoyama style, inspired by Chinese Ming sculpture and architecture. You'd need from dawn to dusk to take in all the detail, a fact that has prompted the Japanese to nickname it the "Twilight Gate".

Off to the left of the Yomeimon is the **Yakushido Temple**, largest at the Toshogu sanctuary, more lavishly decorated than most Japanese Buddhist structures, with its famous ceiling fresco of an angry-looking Naki-ryu, "Crying Dragon", so called because of the shrill reverberation caused by clapping your hands beneath it.

Directly beyond it is the **Karamon** ("Chinese Gate"; note the Chinese sages under the ga-

bles), again festooned with flowers and dragons and a mythical animal, the *tsutsuga*, guardian of all buildings. This is where you take your shoes off and put your camera away before taking the five copper-plated steps to the Honden (Main Hall). Its inner sanctuary contains the golden shrine, **Gokuden**, inhabited by the divine spirits of Ieyasu Tokugawa and those he considered

most worthy to accompany him here, his predecessor Hideyoshi Toyotomi and the great Kamakura shogun Yoritomo Minamoto.

From the not quite sublime but certainly formidably impressive, the tour takes you next to the delightfully frivolous "Gateway of the Sleeping Cat", **Nemurineko**. Snoozing in the eternal summertime of flowering pe-onies, the cat is said to keep all rodents away from the shrine. Legend has it that its sculptor, Jingoro "Left-Handed" Hidari, had a talent so great that his right hand was chopped off by a jealous rival.

The things people say, Toshogu monkeys prefer not to know.

Beyond the Sleeping Cat, the Sakashitamon Gate leads you to the 207 steps that climb—with a resting place halfway up—to the **Tomb of Ieyasu Tokugawa**. The pathway itself is one of the most rewarding moments of the visit. Rising beside a cool stream that rushes back down the hill, the stairway takes you through a veritable cathedral of monumental cedars that prove dear old Matsudaira's contribution more precious than all the gold foil splashed over the Yomeimon and other grand edifices of the sanctuary. At the top, beyond a Hall of Worship and the Inukimon Gate, is the **Hoto**, a miniature bronze pagoda containing the ashes of the great shogun.

The dutiful grandson, Iemitsu Tokugawa, who supervised the building of Toshogu, has his own mausoleum, **Daiyuin**, to the west, opulent in its own way, but on a slightly smaller scale and with more of a Buddhist atmosphere to it.

Walking the trails around the forest and waterfalls in the hilly countryside between Nikko and the resort area of Lake Chuzenji offers a welcome antidote if you feel you've overdosed on the monumental architecture. If you're here for only one day, do at least take a taxi or bus ride from Nikko Station for an easy view of the spectacular winding **Irohazaka Highway** to the lake.

At the western end of the road, you can walk down the hillside (or ride down in an elevator) to the foot of the lovely **Kegon Falls**. The slightest hint of sunshine produces a single and sometimes double rainbow through the spray of the 300-foot (90-m.)-high cascade. Less spectacular, but equally pleasant, are the **Ryuzu Falls** on the north edge of the lake, where you can sit at a teahouse directly overlooking the foot of the falls.

On **Lake Chuzenji** itself, you'll find tour boats and even rowing boats from which you might like to try your hand at trout fishing (rent the tackle and obtain your licence at the lakeside fishing office at Chuzenji-Onsen).

What Barefoot Cheek!
The clash of Japanese culture and Western technology created misunderstandings of positively legendary proportions. Take the opening of Japan's first railway, from Tokyo to Yokohama in 1872. In time-honoured manner, before the Japanese government officials and court dignitaries entered their compartments at Tokyo's Shimbashi Station, they took off their geta clogs. They were apparently somewhat put out to discover that their shoes were not waiting for them to slip into again when they stepped onto the platform at Yokohama.

Yokohama

This once insignificant little fishing village has emerged as a major symbol of Japan's modern confrontation with and triumph over the Western world. With a population fast approaching the 3 million mark, Yokohama has ousted Osaka as Japan's second city. More and more workers and office employees are deserting Tokyo to live in the spacious, relatively uncrowded neighbourhoods of Yokohama, not just because of the cheaper rents, but also for the more human dimension of the housing in a city that has not succumbed to the skyscraper as the only form of 20th-century urban architecture. The town has a cosmopolitan flavour on its waterfront, in the lively Chinatown and around the old "Western" neighbourhoods.

This is the place where in 1854 Commodore Matthew Perry negotiated the Treaty of Kanagawa (a village since swallowed up by Yokohama) to open up to foreign trade the ports of Shimoda, Hakodate and, five years later, Yokohama and many more (see p. 44). To avoid too much contaminating fraternization with the Japanese, the shogun hoped to isolate the new foreign community on the inhospitable mudflats of the bay's right bank— "Yokohama"—just as his ancestors had docked the 17th-century Dutch merchants on the tiny island of Dejima in Nagasaki Bay. But after the Meiji Restoration, the Americans, French and Dutch quickly spread beyond their confinement to high ground still called today the Bluff. The town prospered through commerce in silk and other luxury goods and from the "rest and recreation" provided for tired, frustrated sailors. In World War II, Yokohama was of major strategic importance and a prime target for the American bombs which completely wiped out the harbour in 1945. It was hastily restored to service for the United States Navy in the Korean War and is today Japan's number one trading port and among the most important in the world.

Take the Japan Railways (JR) Keihin-Tohoku Line from Tokyo Yurakucho Station, 40 minutes to Sakuragicho, Yokohama's port-side station. (The faster *shinkansen* leaves you stranded on the city outskirts.)

From Sakuragicho, it's just a short walk to the waterfront— foreign residents still call it by its old "Western imperialist" name of the **Bund**, as in Shanghai. Start your tour at the South Pier, Osambashi, for a good view of the giant oil tankers, freighters and luxury ocean liners that dock in Yokohama from all over the world. You can take a 50-minute tour of the harbour on one of the motorboats moored beside the old 1930s liner *Hikawa Maru* (now retired from service, but equipped with some nice tropical fish aquariums and a youth hostel).

At the entrance to the South Pier is the nine-storey **Silk Centre**. Its Silk Museum has a superb kimono collection; and you can stop in for a look at the trading on the Silk Exchange.

The waterfront **Yamashita Park** is a favourite of painters and fishermen. The area behind the park, Yamashita-cho, is the old centre of Japan's first foreign consulates and trade missions; most of them are still there, imparting a distinctly 19th-century atmosphere.

For a bird's-eye view of the harbour, take the elevator to the top of the 348-foot (106-m.) **Marine Tower** at the south-east corner of Yamashita Park. It serves as a lighthouse at the top and houses an interesting oceanography museum.

Like many good port-cities around the world, Yokohama has a thriving **Chinatown**—Chukagai to the Japanese—bright with neon lights on its shops and restaurants, although the couple of old-time opium dens still in business do not advertise themselves.

Motomachi is a high-class shopping district, selling luxury goods at lower prices than you'll find on the Ginza in Tokyo. It separates Chinatown from the Westerners' favourite residential area, the **Bluff** (or Yamate-machi). Take a pleasant stroll among the European-style houses, schools and churches. It's surprising how quaint they seem in the Japanese setting.

The attractive little **Yamate Museum** recalls the history of Yokohama's foreign community. There's also a picturesque **International Cemetery**, notably last resting place for two much admired Victorian English gentlemen: engineer Edmund Morell (d. 1871) who helped build the Tokyo-Yokohama Railway, and Charles Wirgman (d. 1891), a cartoonist for the *Illustrated London News*, who had the comical idea of creating the now also defunct satirical magazine, *Japan Punch*. If you don't find such places too spooky, the cemetery's a great vantage point for the evening panorama of the illuminated harbour.

You can also rest your sightseeing legs at the south-east edge of town in the lovely **Sankeien Gardens**, laid out by a wealthy silk merchant of the Meiji era. At great expense, he transferred two important 17th-century houses that once belonged to the Tokugawa family, the charming Choshukaku teahouse and the Rinshunkaku country villa, both well worth a visit.

Kamakura

One of the key cities of Japan's history, Kamakura has experienced a destiny the very opposite of nearby Yokohama's. Whereas the latter grew from a little fishing village to one of the most important seaports in the world, Kamakura began life in the 12th century as the seat of government of the first of the mighty Japanese shoguns and ended up a couple of centuries later as just another little fishing village.

Today Kamakura is a place of pilgrimage for visitors paying homage to the memory of the great Yoritomo Minamoto (see p. 32) and for Tokyo residents seeking a day of rest at the seaside.

Minamoto set up his government at Kamakura in 1192 because he wanted to remove his political and military advisers from the debilitating influence of the soft life at the imperial capital of Kyoto. Today, Kamakura's sandy beaches and mellow climate have made it a very desirable commuter town for businessmen escaping the hard, stressful life of the modern capital of Tokyo.

The warriors who began at Kamakura the military rule of Japan that was to remain unbroken until the 19th century were profoundly religious men. The dominant spiritual influence of the time was Zen Buddhism, and Kamakura still has dozens of the Buddhist temples to which the samurai used to retreat for meditation after—or prior to—the turmoil of battle. Businessmen have now replaced the samurai, while tourists flock to admire the gigantic Daibutsu ("Great Buddha") in one of the temples.

We recommend a route that, rather than plunging into the main tourist attraction at once, leads you gently to the crowds around the Daibutsu. Get off the train at the north end of town, Kita-Kamakura Station (one hour from Tokyo Station on the Yokosuka line). Here you are within easy walking distance of the first of the interesting temples—or else you can hire a taxi at the station if you're also heading for some of the more remote and less-crowded temples up on the lovely wooded hillsides.

But take time, too, to walk around the town, through its narrow streets and alleyways, and peek through the bamboo fences at some of the exquisite **miniature gardens** in the residential neighbourhoods. Better than most of what you're likely to see in Tokyo, these will give you some idea of the atmosphere of the "good old days".

First stop from Kita-Kamakura Station is the **Engakuji Temple**. Its Shariden Hall is one of the few Kamakura religious buildings to have escaped the 1923 earthquake, a valuable example of the sober style of Zen architecture. It contains a quartz reliquary (*sharideni*) said to contain one of Buddha's many teeth housed in sanctuaries throughout the Buddhist world. The temple gardens, surrounded by dense groves of imposing Japanese cedars, offer a delightful leisurely walk. In the Butsunichian Teahouse, once a shogun's villa, take a sip or two of the thick green tea. If it's too bitter for you, suck it through one of the pink or blue bird-shaped sweets. The garden-terraces give you a superb view down to the Nameri River valley.

Downhill from Engakuji, you pass the Tokeiji Temple. Nothing special to visit, but noteworthy as the "Divorce Temple" created at the end of the 13th century to provide a sanctuary for women persecuted by cruel husbands or mothers-in-law. If they stayed three years in the temple's convent, they obtained an automatic divorce. You may still see Buddhist nuns today, but they are silent on their reasons for being there.

The Japanese like to classify their monuments, grouping them according to historic and artistic importance, and if Kamakura is said to have Five Great Zen Temples (as well as Ten Clear Wells, for instance), the

Kenchoji—15 minutes' walk from Tokeiji—is regarded as Number One. It was founded in 1253 for a Chinese monk, Tao Lung, who interceded with the dreaded Kublai Khan to stop the Mongols invading Japan. Fire and civil war took their toll on the original buildings, but today's structures are faithful renderings of the original Kamakura style. The great bronze bell, over 700 years old, remained intact. In the main hall is a fine sandalwood sculpture of the Hojo regent who founded the temple—much more realistic in its features than the over-stylized work of the late Heian period of the Kyoto court, epitomizing the new no-nonsense attitudes introduced by the Kamakura regime.

Most beautiful of the more secluded temples is the **Zuisenji**. The garden with its rock pool and evergreens is the perfect setting for quiet meditation. Many of the monasteries in these temples offer initiation into Zen Buddhism for the layman with English-speaking monks.

Tough old Yoritomo Minamoto's great monument is the **Tsurugaoka Hachimangu Shrine**. Actually it is formally dedicated to

Kamakura's Great Buddha meditates beyond any earthly paradise.

an ancient 3rd-century emperor, but Minamoto appropriated it for his short-lived dynasty, Hachiman being to his liking as the great God of War. The Shinto shrine and its lotus pond are popular now with Japanese visitors, particularly for the fine **view** over Kamakura's Sagami Bay. In mid-September a splendid tournament of archery on horseback, *yabusame*, is held at the shrine festival. This exciting sport in Kamakura-era costume demands that each archer hit as many targets as possible while galloping past at full tilt.

The **Tomb of Yoritomo Minamoto** is a very modest affair, characteristic of his austere regime—compare the Tokugawa mausoleums at Nikko. You can see the little moss-covered stone pagoda marking his grave east of the Hachimangu Shrine.

The considerable artistic achievements of his era and the somewhat bolder Muromachi period that followed can be seen at the **Kamakura Municipal Museum**, just down the hill from the Hachimangu Shrine. The museum houses art treasures from the Kamakura temples and shrines. Outstanding among the sculptures is a statue of Shigefusa Uyesugi, leading counsellor to the shogun, wearing an almost painful expression typifying the world-weary politician. There are also some excellent 13th-century paintings, including a subtle portrait of the Chinese monk Tao Lung.

The **Daibutsu** is Kamakura's most celebrated monument. Situated in the grounds of the Kotokuin Temple on the south-west side of town, the massive bronze seated statue of the Buddha is 37 feet (11.4 m.) tall, second in size only to a Buddha at Nara's Todaiji Temple, but considered artistically greatly superior. The pose with the hands resting on his lap, the thumbs touching the palms, the eyes half-closed, expresses the spiritual state of

---

Shizuka's Dance

The Hachimangu Shrine was the scene of many dramatic incidents, including the assassination of a shogun by his nephew, the shrine's high priest—a great gingko tree marks the spot where the perfidious priest was hiding. But most poignant of all was the story of Shizuka, lissome mistress of Yoritomo Minamoto's uppity brother Yoshitsune. Yoshitsune's bravery and popularity as a warrior posed a threat to the shogun, who sought to eliminate him by cunning. Yoritomo rather sadistically made Shizuka dance for him at Hachimangu Shrine while trying to find out from her where he could hunt down her lover. It is not recorded whether she "sang" as well as danced.

peace purified of all worldly desires that is the goal of the Buddhist doctrine.

The statue is hollow inside and you can climb a staircase to look out through a window between the Buddha's shoulders. The carnival-like atmosphere surrounding the statue diminishes once you're inside. In the dark you may miss a sign proclaiming in English: "Stranger, whosoever thou art and whatsoever be thy creed, when thou enterest this sacred statue, remember that this is a *tathogata garba*, the womb of cosmical body, and should therefore be entered with reverence, not contamination".

Nearby is the **Hase Kannon**, temple of the gilded wooden 11-headed female embodiment of mercy and a popular pilgrimage for the faithful. As you approach the main hall, you'll pass hundreds of small grey stone statues of Jizo, guardian divinity of children, each festooned with the children's offerings of glass beads, toy cars, plastic windmills, even packets of chewing gum.

Time for the **beach**. In spring and summer, the crowds head for Yuigahama and Shichirigahama beaches. Brave the mob scene to see the schoolgirls venture into the water with their immaculate navy blue uniforms hugged around their knees. If you want to swim yourself, your best bet is after September 1. That's the end of summer for the Japanese and however warm it may still be, they just seem to stop going to the beach. From Shichirigahama at the south-west end of town, you get a good view of Mt. Fuji. As we told you in Tokyo, don't knock it, you may not see Fuji when you get up close.

Hakone

To the Japanese the Fuji-Hakone-Izu region, comprising the country's most sacred and celebrated mountain, tranquil lakes, hot spring spas and seaside resorts, is one large vacation area. Just one hour and a half from Tokyo, the Hakone resort area makes a very pleasant day trip. But a good alternative, if you want to take it easy and enjoy a little more of the countryside, is to stay overnight and continue down the Izu Peninsula the next day.

Even if you have a precious Japan Railpass, we suggest for the day trip that you forsake the JR for once and take advantage of the deal offered by the Odakyu Railway. The variety of rides you get is more than half the fun. For an all-in fare, you get the "Hakone Free Pass" which includes a return (round-trip) train ticket from Shinjuku linking up with the local Hakone funicular railway up the mountain to a cable car. This swings you across the Owakudani volcanic landscape and down the other side for a boat cruise across Lake Ashi to Hakone-machi resort. Here you take the bus along the Sukumo River to Odawara Station and return by train to Tokyo.

This is a mountain region and so always a little cooler than Tokyo—even in summer you should take a sweater for the evening. The funicular railway takes you up through larch and pine forests, in and out of narrow tunnels past rocky torrents and the hot spring spa of Miyanoshita to the Gora terminus. Here you walk through a charming little rock park to what must be one of the world's most spectacular sculpture gardens, the **Hakone Open Air Museum** (also known as Chokoku-no-Mori, "Forest of Sculptures"). In an emerald green alpine meadow perched on the mountainside, it provides a magnificent marriage of striking monumental 20th-century Western and Japanese sculptures with a wonderfully arranged free-form landscape. As lovely as it is in spring and summer, for many it's even more beautiful in the snows of winter (practically all the outdoor exhibits are chosen for their resistance to the elements). It's a delight to rediscover Henry

Moore, Giacometti, Barbara Hepworth and Alexander Calder in a Japanese setting alongside their Japanese contemporaries such as Kotaro Takamura, Takashi Shimizu and Masashi Seki. Children love this museum because they can climb all over many of the art works unhindered by signs warning them not to touch.

Tear yourself away and take the cable car up across the

desolate volcanic terrain of Mt. Kamiyama to **Owakudani**. With belching yellow sulphurous fumes far below you, this looks like a dismal cold inferno imagined by some Dante of the tundra. The Owakudani Natural Science Museum has some fascinating audio-visual presentations of volcanic eruptions. Push the button for some great sound effects and then go down to the basement where the seismographs scratch

There's more than one way to get across the lovely Lake Ashi.

away, silently tracing the earth's heartbeat.

Another cable car takes you down to a harbour where a three-masted pleasure boat painted a gay red, blue and gold and reassuringly named *Victoria* awaits you. The 20-minute cruise across pretty **Lake Ashi** to Hakone-machi—some good fishing for trout and bass for anyone staying longer—ends, invariably, with the ship's loudspeakers blaring a scratchy version of *Auld Lang Syne*. This is a favourite tune of the Japanese and many of them are disappointed to discover it is Scottish. In early August, the lake resorts stage the dramatic night-time *Torii Matsuri* festival, when a great wooden *torii* is set alight and a thousand burning lanterns are sent floating out across the water.

Hakone-machi is a resort town noteworthy to the casual visitor principally for its souvenir shops

Hakone open-air sculpture garden makes artful use of landscape.

selling *Hakone-zaiku*, much admired wooden articles of inlaid mosaic and marquetry.

In the days when the Tokugawa held sway, the **Hakone Barrier** (five minutes' lakeside walk from Hakone-machi) was one of the most important checkpoints on the great Tokaido toll road. This was the route the *daimyo* had to take from Kyoto to the capital for their

tribute to the shogun (see p. 40). A replica of the guardhouse, manned by costumed figures of the old feudal era, has been constructed, while the nearby Hakone Museum displays relics of the time including swords, spears, halberds and European muskets.

Izu Peninsula

Izu Peninsula (one hour on the *shinkansen* bullet train from Tokyo to the town of Atami) is another popular vacation spot for Tokyoites fleeing the metropolis. It's blessed with a sunny climate, some fine swimming beaches and romantic bays for fishing or just lazing around in a boat.

Two of the resort towns are of considerable historic interest to Westerners. On the east coast, **Ito**, a hot spring spa with good surf swimming and some hunting in the pretty hills behind the town, was the home for a while of William Adams (1564–1620), English seaman and adviser to Ieyasu Tokugawa. It was here that Adams—the model for the hero of James Clavell's novel *Shogun**—set up his shipyard to build Japan's first European-

---

*This popular best seller in the West has been received with some ambivalence in Japan. It has attracted more tourists, but is also widely regarded as a distorted portrayal of Japanese life of the period.

style, ocean-going ships—not too many, though, because Tokugawa did not want his warriors commandeering them to leave the country and return with foreign invaders. You'll find an **Adams Monument** at the mouth of the Okawa River, just over a mile south-east of Ito Station, celebrating the man known to the Japanese as Anjin Miura.

At the southern end of the peninsula, **Shimoda** is famous as America's first foothold in Japan. The **Gyokusenji Temple** was where Townsend Harris hoisted the Star-Spangled Banner to set up the U.S. Consulate in 1856. The temple still displays some of Harris's personal belongings. The most intriguing monument here is the **Butchered Cow Tree**, commemorating the spot where a cow was slaughtered to provide Harris with his first steak dinner in Japan. This so horrified the Japanese peasants, who did not yet eat meat, that they hid away their cattle in case the habit spread—beef *sukiyaki* was still a long way off.

In fact, charming as it still is today as a fishing and sailing harbour, Shimoda proved absolutely worthless as a trading port—Tokugawa had just stuck the Americans there to keep them away from his capital—so Harris negotiated to open up Yokohama to foreign trade two years later. Now, in May, Shimoda's *Kurofune Matsuri* (Black Ship Festival) celebrates the coming of what were known as the "Black Ships" of the United States Navy.

Mt. Fuji

While most of the civilized world's national symbols are man-made—America's Statue of Liberty, Britain's Houses of Parliament, France's Eiffel Tower or Russia's Kremlin—Japan's is a phenomenon of nature. And yet, in its almost perfect symmetry, the volcanic cone of Mt. Fuji—Fujiyama to the Japanese —snowcapped even in midsummer, is so exquisitely formed as to seem, like so much Japanese landscape, the work of an artist rather than of nature. Here, more than in any temple garden or old castle grounds, you can appreciate why the Japanese themselves prefer to blur the distinction between nature and art.

Mt. Fuji constitutes the dream and paramount destination of countless Japanese pilgrims—many saving up for a lifetime to travel at least once to this hallowed peak looming 12,388 feet (3,776 m.) into the heavens. Fed by the national Shinto cult's worship of nature and the Buddhist view of mountains as a sacred cosmos, the people's feelings for *Fuji-san* are a mixture of piety and marvelling pride. (Official

Japanese descriptions nonetheless graciously couple their pride and joy with Ecuador's Mt. Cotopaxi as "the world's two most beautiful conical volcanoes".)

Until the Meiji Restoration, women were not allowed to approach its slopes. Now over 400,000 men and women climb the mountain every year. For some, it is revered as the seat of the nation's ancestral deities, an abode for the souls of the dead, for others, climbing it is the ideal performance of Buddhism's ascetic exercises of self-discipline and physical purification. Others come without any religious belief at all to experience the mountain's ineffable beauty and leave, almost despite themselves, with a keen sense of spiritual uplift. No travel brochure can dim the ultimate impact of Mt. Fuji nor the most blasé of world travellers remain immune.

The volcano's name is thought to derive from an Ainu word for "fire". It last erupted in 1707, and today only an occasional puff of steam bursts through its crust, the fitful snore of a sleeping giant. It is set in the appropriately serene landscape of its Five Lakes, waterfalls and dark forest.

The challenge of Fuji is to reach its peak in time to watch the rising sun, that other symbol of Japan. In fine weather, this experience is all it was ever cracked up to be. The official climbing season, when mountain huts at ten stations along each of the routes are open to lodge the pilgrims, is from July 1 to August 31, but other expeditions, recommended for experienced climbers only, continue all year round. (If you can't actually climb to the top, it's still well worth your while visiting the lower slopes and surroundings.) The Japanese traditionally dress all in white for the Fuji ascent, with straw sandals covering their climbing shoes. It would not be considered misplaced for you to do the same.

You must count on five to nine hours to reach the summit and three to five hours for the descent. To see *goraiko*, as the sunrise at the summit is known, you can either start late afternoon and climb all night—cool but not dangerous—or stop off at the seventh or eighth station to rest and resume your climb to get to the top before dawn. From Tokyo a 2½-hour bus journey from the Shinjuku bus terminal takes you up to the fifth station (climbing time is calculated from there).

Bad junk food from vending machines is all that's available at the top—along with a litter problem we can only pray the authorities can some day overcome—so it's best to take your own little

*Rowing enhances its elegance
in the sacred shadow of Mt. Fuji.*

picnic, and above all a flask of hot tea or coffee.

There are six different trails to the top. The preferred trail for people coming from Tokyo—the one the Shinjuku bus takes you to—is the north face's **Kawaguchiko**, from which you get a view of the Fuji Five Lakes and the Japan Alps. If you're coming from Kyoto or Osaka, the train or bus takes you to the **Fujinomiya** trail (also to the fifth station) on the south face, with a view of the Pacific.

At the top: **goraiko** and the changes of colour from purple to scarlet to shining copper to ice blue, culminating in the triumphant gold of the climbing sun.

You should not confine your visit just to the mountain. The

Fuji Five Lakes that describe a crescent around the north side of the volcano offer exhilarating separate excursions, with opportunities for hunting, fishing and hiking. Each lake has its own characteristics. From east to west: Yamanaka is the biggest; Kawaguchi is the most popular, probably because its north shore gives you a perfect reflection of Mt. Fuji for a double-image photograph; Saiko offers the best trout fishing; Shoji is in itself the most picturesque, with the added attraction for photographers of nearby Mt. Eboshi providing the most satisfying view of Fuji (non-photographers are also permitted); Motosu is the deepest and bluest.

Between Lakes Saiko and Shoji is the beautiful dense primeval forest of **Jukai**, ''Sea of Trees''. A walk here provides a wonderful moment of peace, but be careful how you make your way in and out, because the presence of volcanic lava makes a magnetic compass useless in finding your bearings. In recent years, unhappy Japanese lovers have often chosen Jukai for one last tryst before sealing a suicide pact in its impenetrable heart.

Due south of Lake Motosu, the more cheerful, glistening white **Shiraito Waterfall**, only 85 feet (26 m.) high but five times as wide, makes the perfect backdrop for a picnic.

KINKI

Embracing Kyoto and Nara, the Ise-Shima shrines, the city of Osaka and port of Kobe, the Kinki region is quite simply the heart of the nation's culture. While Tokyo can exhilarate with its somewhat crude vigour, Kyoto impresses with its refinement. Nara remains venerable as the first important home of the imperial court and its temples. Ise-Shima National Park is the picturesque sanctuary of Japan's ancestral deities. Osaka and Kobe bustle and burst with the dynamism of the country's commercial present and future. Since Japanese rulers always planned their cities and shrines with a deliberate eye to the beauty of the surrounding landscape, you can rest assured that you will be visiting the region's monuments in exquisite settings. And the cities also offer some great entertainment as a bonus.

Kyoto

If you cannot understand a country's present without first understanding its past, Tokyo means nothing without Kyoto. Kyoto is Japan's Athens, its Paris, Rome and Jerusalem, for a thousand years the cultural and spiritual capital of Japanese civilization, the home of its revered emperors from the end of the 8th century to the Meiji Restoration. Kyoto just means ''Capital City'', though it was first known as Heian-kyo—"Capital of Peace"—which gave its name to the golden Heian era from the 10th to the 12th centuries.

Whatever measures the country's military rulers took to divert the political power-centre away from the imperial court—first to Kamakura, later to Edo—Kyoto remained the repository of the nation's noblest aspirations. (It was the one major Japanese city that American scholars were able to persuade the United States Air Force *not* to bomb in World War II. What destruction its monuments have suffered has been from fire and medieval civil strife.)

Sanzen-in's temple-garden in Kyoto is a haven for meditation.

Just as no shogun dared rule without at least the symbolic blessing of the emperor, so no palace, shrine or temple could be built in the shogun's capital without the expertise of the architects, artists and craftsmen of imperial Kyoto. Until the 19th century, Kyoto remained the principal home of Japan's poets, priests and scholars (and is still today, with Tokyo, the major university centre of the country). The soldiers and politicians learned calligraphy, the tea ceremony, indeed all their manners from the monks and courtiers of Kyoto. Their ladies took their cues from Kyoto for the proper forms for their kimono, their make-up, flower arrangements, and the superb court-inspired cuisine. To please her man, the geisha of Osaka or Edo took tips from the geisha of Kyoto—and, once again, Kyoto remains the last true bastion of authentic geisha girls, with two schools still open to train novices (see p. 190).

But there's no reason to be daunted by the sheer wealth of Kyoto's cultural heritage. The town is a lot of fun, too. True, there are over 1,500 Buddhist temples and 200 Shinto shrines—on the other hand, only three palaces and nine museums (since each temple's treasure house is a museum in its own right). Obviously, you will want to visit only a tiny fraction of these—there's so much else to see, too.

The town's traditional craftsmen are still there, most of them descendants of those who built the original temples and palaces and are called upon today to do the work of restoration and reconstruction—you'll stumble upon stone masons, carpenters and other artisans in their back alley workshops behind the tem-

Handling Kyoto

The golden rule to abide by in Kyoto: dose your sightseeing—visit a temple or two, rest in the gardens, explore the back streets, take time off for a leisurely Japanese tea, investigate the lively nightlife, take a couple of hours over dinner. And if your mind is still suffering from an overload of cultural "input", give it a rest with the nicely stultifying pleasures of pachinko (see p. 187)—Kyoto is the perfect place in which to initiate yourself into this idiotic game's arcane joys. Crowds are a problem almost everywhere, but the best way to avoid them is to do your main sightseeing early morning and late afternoon.

The shinkansen gets you into Kyoto from Tokyo in under three hours; you'll know you're arriving by the little old Buddhist temple wedged in between two sets of railway lines as you approach Kyoto Station—those temples are just everywhere. If you're not too tired to do anything but check into your hotel, start by collecting information, maps and brochures from the admirable TIC located on the ground floor of the Kyoto Tower at the beginning of the Karasuma-dori, the main thoroughfare leading directly from Kyoto Station. (While you're there, take the elevator up the 430-foot (131-m.) "space needle" tower for your first view of the city.)

Study your literature well before venturing out on your first exploration of Kyoto. Here, more than anywhere in Japan, that notebook we recommended will be useful for jotting down your choice among all those temples and other monuments, where they're situated, which bus route, and so on.

Public transport in Kyoto is good. A subway line runs north-south from Kyoto Station and another is planned for the east-west axis. Otherwise, it's best to use the bus service and show the bus driver where you want to get off (the next pages will indicate the route numbers and bus stop names). In some cases, you may prefer to hire a taxi for a half-day to take you to several temples in the same neighbourhood.

But be ready to do some walking, with plenty of rest stops planned in between. Kyoto is a town that really repays casual exploration. We can indicate a few of the pleasures, but in Kyoto your most faithful companion will be "serendipity"—the joy of coming across a thing of beauty by sheer accident.

ples. You can see silk-weavers and embroiderers preparing the beautiful materials that make up the kimono wardrobe of any self-respecting matron or bride-to-be. Dolls, ceramics, porcelain, fine silk or paper fans, lacquerware and bambooware are all still manufactured in Kyoto by the artisans who have for centuries enjoyed the imperial family's seal of approval—like those working "By Appointment" to the crowned heads of Europe.

Imperial Residences

Three of the principal sights in Kyoto—the Katsura and Shugakuin Imperial Villas and the Imperial Palace (Kyoto Gosho)—are such a "hot ticket" with Japanese visitors that you have to book ahead with the Kyoto office of the Imperial Household Agency to get in. How much in advance varies from season to season, but the JNTO in Tokyo can advise you on how to go about it before you leave for Kyoto (no overseas applications). Foreign visitors are given priority over the Japanese, who sometimes have a waiting list of months. If you can visit only one of the superbly designed villas, Katsura is well worth the effort and the palace is of considerable interest to those who would like to compare the simple dignity with which latterday emperors lived to the grandeur of the shoguns.

Imperial Palace (2 miles [3½ km.] north of Kyoto Station, subway to Imadegawa Station). Fires took their toll of the original 8th-century palace, and the present buildings are a 19th-century reconstruction on the site of the palace of 1790. Entrance for the guided tour is through the western Seishomon Gate. You will visit the Shishinden ceremonial hall, draped in elegant silks and decorated with the gilded 16-petalled imperial chrysanthemum. This was where the emperor was enthroned at the beginning of his reign—a privilege retained by Kyoto after the move to Tokyo—and held his New Year's audiences. To the west is the cypress-wood Seiryoden, "Serene and Cool Chamber", the emperor's private chapel, serene and cool indeed in vermilion, white and black. The imperial dais is flanked by two wooden *koma-inu* liondogs, traditional guardians of all Shinto shrines.

Katsura Imperial Villa (3 miles [5 km.] west of Kyoto Station on the Hankyu Railway to Katsura Station) is one of Japan's masterpieces of residential design and garden landscaping. It was commissioned for Prince Toshihito, brother of the emperor, in 1590, as a generous gesture of Hideyoshi. Master landscaper Enshu Kobori insisted he have as much time and money as the project needed and that no one peep until the villa and gardens were completed—well into the next century.

All the "walls" of the villa's seven pavilions are in fact sliding panels to be opened for surveying the surrounding landscape, both the gardens themselves and the Arashiyama Hills beyond. The Furushoin Pavilion verandah is the perfect place for viewing the full moon. Interior panels are decorated with the paintings of the celebrated Kano school. The "strolling" gardens, with their central pond and teahouses, are beautifully arranged with a rich use of different coloured mosses, and exquisite miniature maple trees border streams channelled from the nearby Katsura River. Conceived with meticulous care, Katsura is all artful simplicity, which the Japanese like to contrast with the extravaganzas being built over roughly the same period by the Tokugawa shoguns at Nikko.

Shugakuin Imperial Villa (6 miles [10 km.] north-east of Kyoto Station; buses 5 or 35 to Shugakuin-michi stop, then a 15-minute signposted walk). At the foot of sacred Mt. Hiei, the spacious grounds are a splendid example of the "strolling" gardens favoured in the Tokugawa Edo period. Built by the shogun in the 17th century for an abdicated emperor, Shugakuin is in fact three villas, each with airy summer-style open teahouses in the gardens. The Middle Villa includes

Entering womanhood is the occasion of a solemn ceremony for Kyoto girls.

a temple built for the ex-Emperor's daughter, a Buddhist nun, and has a delicately landscaped garden with pond and waterfall. The Upper Villa, grandest of the three, dominates an imposing avenue of pines. Tiers of shrubs lead up to the Rinun-tei, a summer pavilion with a superb view over Kyoto.

After these visits involving special arrangements, you can divide your tour of Kyoto into neighbourhoods:

Higashiyama

On the city's east side, Higashiyama is a fascinating mixture of temples, theatre district, museums and parks, the most delightful area in which to start your walking tours.

Take the 206 bus to the Kiyomizu-michi stop and head up the hill just 10 minutes towards **Kiyomizu Temple**, probably the most popular in all Kyoto. (Resist the lively shopping district

that borders the temple approach until after you've visited the temple.) The thatched and tiled roofs of the 17th-century temple (reconstructed from an 8th-century structure founded at the same time as the imperial capital itself) are tiered like terraces on Higashiyama Hill in a dramatic landscape of cliffs and waterfalls. The hill itself shimmers pink and silver with the cherry blossoms of spring or the ruddy

Kiyomizu Temple offers food for thought, but pigeons are interested in something more tangible.

glow of maple leaves in autumn, but the brilliant rich greens of the rest of the year are just as rewarding, especially in late afternoon. Give yourself plenty of time to stroll around the temple grounds.

The Hondo Main Hall, has a broad wooden terrace jutting out

over the valley. Looking across the valley with a three-storey pagoda on the other side and down across the city, the effect is quite dizzying. Indeed, the Japanese use the expression "Jump from the Kiyomizu verandah" to mean doing something daring and irrevocable.

Now you can backtrack down the hill past the shops selling food, fans, masks, porcelain bells, dolls, necklaces, embroidered silk bags—both souvenir junk and exquisite craftsmanship, so look carefully. The artisans' workshops are away from the main temple street, down back alleys, one of which has kept its nickname provided by the first British visitors in the 19th century: Teapot Lane, for the first-rate porcelain and ceramics. Behind some of the elegant little shops you may be lucky enough to find a garden where the owner will serve you some tea—an irresistible sales pitch for his cups and plates.

Walk north along Sannenzaka Street and then turn west past the five-storey Yasaka Pagoda to the area known as **Gion**. This is Kyoto's main theatre and entertainment district, home of the geishas.

At the Kaburenjo Theatre, if you're here in April or May, you can see the *miyako odori*, "Cherry Dance", to traditional instruments—the three-stringed and water garden of Kamakura's Zuisenji Temple.

The Zen garden reached its purest expression in Kyoto with the hiraniwa, "flat gardens", devoid of hills, bridges or ponds, just an arrangement of rocks in white sand or gravel. The most famous is at Ryoanji Temple, but equally admirable examples can be seen at Nanzenji's "Leaping Tiger Garden" or Zuiho-in's "Blissful Mountain".

More elaborate designs were evolved to incorporate existing natural features in the plan, as in the large ornate pond-gardens at the Ginkakuji (Silver Pavilion) or the Kinkakuji (Golden Pavilion). The opulent Momoyama architecture at the end of the 16th century brought with it gardens of appropriately dramatic character, high in colour with bizarrely shaped rocks and tree formations, as at Kyoto's Nishi-Honganji Temple.

The popularity of the tea ceremony led to the incorporation of the teahouse in garden landscaping, usually designed by the tea master himself in a secluded area partitioned off from the rest of the garden. The essential element here is a sense of detachment from the outside world, with perhaps some moss-covered stones to evoke a romantic air of neglect and a winding path to conceal the teahouse entrance.

The Edo period of the Tokugawa shoguns took the job of garden landscaping out of the hands of amateur aesthetes, monks and tea masters and handed it to professionals, who brought together all the elements of existing designs. The acknowledged master gardener of this era was Enshu Kobori, whose work can be seen at the Katsura Imperial Villa and the temples of Daitokuji, Kodaiji and Nanzenji. The major new idea was the concept of shakkei, "borrowed landscape", laying out the garden to include in the total design distant views of, say, Mt. Fuji, a forest or the sea.

Edo garden design became more utilitarian, with fruit trees to provide food and reeds for making arrows. Larger so-called "strolling" gardens came close to the spirit of English parks, but still with very deliberate aesthetic touches, such as in the celebrated Kenrokuen Gardens of Kanazawa or the Ritsurin Park of Takamatsu on Shikoku island.

And Japanese gardens have something even for our industrial age. At workbenches in the factories, you can see bonkei tray-gardens with miniature bonsai trees, pebble-rocks, and even a tiny goldfish pond. The equivalent in the cities' crowded tenements are the hako-niwa box-gardens. Technicians are now working on cosmic gardens for the first Japanese space vessel.

samisen, flute and drums. The 17th-century Minamiza Theatre, oldest in Japan, features the famous Kaomise Kabuki show in December.

But for foreign visitors, an institution named **Gion Corner** is there, in Yasaka Hall, to provide you with a smorgasbord—or perhaps we should say "sushi-tray" —of Japanese culture from March 1 to November 29. In a comfortable little theatre you can see a one-hour demonstration of the tea ceremony, traditional music and dance, flower arrangement, *bunraku* puppet drama, and a *kyogen* farce. This may at first seem a little artificial, but in fact the samples are authentically performed by first-class artists. Japanese theatre, music and etiquette are truly so very different from what you may be used to in the West that Gion Corner provides a good introduction for people without the leisure to experience them in a full-length version in their traditional setting, especially if you have difficulty getting tickets or aren't in Japan at the right time for the limited theatre seasons. (Tickets for Gion Corner are usually available through your hotel or the TIC.)

Just west of Gion, on the other bank of the Kamo River, nightlife really hums along **Pontocho** alley between the Sanjo and Shijo bridges. Pontocho is famous for its *ochaya* teahouses frequented by geisha girls, but also for the plentiful other bars and nightclubs.

At the north-east corner of Gion is the Maruyama Park, a popular recreation area for Kyoto citizens, but also containing two important temples. The great **Chion-in Temple**, one of the biggest in Japan, is the home of the Jodo ("Pure Land") sect which in the 12th century spread the appeal of Buddhism to the uneducated classes by declaring it possible to enter the Pure Land just by repeating as often as possible the prayer formula—*Namu-Amida-Butsu*—to the Supreme Buddha. Standing right behind the temple's Main Hall, you can see a statue of the man who first proclaimed this precept, Honen, which he himself carved. The much revered Sammon entrance gate is 78 feet (24 m.) high. Such is the national importance of the Chion-in that the Main Hall is known as the "Hall of One Thousand Tatami Mats", though in fact there are only 360.

A short walk to the north, the **Shoren-in Temple** is famous for its gardens designed by two master landscapers, Soami and Enshu Kobori, providing a lovely framework for the temple's tea pavilion.

At the northern edge of Higashiyama, there's a delightful

walk to be had, most of it along a canal that will take you to two major temples, Nanzenji and Ginkakuji. But before you set out on the walk, you might like to visit two interesting museums displaying Kyoto's age-old supremacy in craftsmanship (both near Higashiyama-Nijo bus stop with the 206 bus).

The **Museum of Traditional Industry** is an attractive modern building with spacious exhibitions of textiles, porcelain, cutlery, lacquerware, fans, dolls and cabinetwork, all accompanied by occasional demonstrations by professional craftsmen.

Next door the **National Museum of Modern Art** is in fact de-

Track down the legendary, elusive geisha girl in Gion or Pontocho.

voted principally to ceramics of the 19th and 20th centuries, with special place being given to work of the Kyoto master Kanjiro Kawai.

Nanzenji is a fine Zen Buddhist temple, formerly a 13th-century palace which Emperor Kameyama (1249-1305) offered to his great Zen master Daimin Kokushi. The precincts house a dozen affiliated temples and monasteries, one of them, the Konchi-in, being open to the public for lay initiation and meditation. The great Sammon gate at the main entrance was built in 1628 and became notorious as the site where a robber named Goemon Ishikawa was boiled alive in an iron vat while holding his son aloft to save him from the same fate. Since then, certain Japanese hot tubs are popularly known as *goemon-burro*. You can climb to the top of the 98-foot (30-m.) -high gate for a fine overall view of the temple grounds and sacred Mt. Hiei to the north.

More in keeping with the peace of mind that Nanzenji generally evokes is the lovely Leaping Tiger Garden that you can view from the terrace of the Main Hall left of the entrance. There's an intriguingly studied casualness, almost neglect, to the arrangement of rocks, trees and shrubs amid the meticulously raked white gravel. It was designed by the Tokugawa shoguns'

favourite master gardener Enshu Kobori.

In the Shohojo ("Superior's Quarters"), look out for the lively 17th-century tiger painting on sliding screens by Tanyu Kano. Notice, too, as you walk in the temple grounds, the intricate system of bamboo conduits carrying water around the gardens with one tube occasionally overbalancing into another with a gentle clap designed to frighten off wild deer that might endanger the shrubs.

Just north-east of Nanzenji, beside the Eikando Temple, begins the **Philosopher's Walk** where Kitaro Nishida, a celebrated philosophy professor at Kyoto University, used to take his daily walk along a little canal bordered by cherry trees and maples. Perfect for your own deeper—or shallower—thoughts, with a stop at one of the teahouses or coffee shops along the way. At the northern end of the canal, you branch off to the east, to the temple of **Ginkakuji**, a 15th-century "Silver Pavilion" that in fact never got round to being covered in the intended silver leaf. Its builder was aesthete-mystic shogun Yoshimasa Ashikaga, who used it as a villa for his esoteric ceremonies of incense burning, tea and, above all, moon-watching in the marvellously elegant garden designed by Soami. Its flat-topped hillock of white gravel, inevitably compared by the Japanese to Mt. Fuji, is said to have originated as a pile of sand left there by Ginka-kuji construction workers.

The 206 bus takes you down to the **Kyoto National Museum**, housing the country's most important collection of Japanese sculpture and painting. The museum rotates its exhibitions of major pieces among its several thousand works assembled from the temples and palaces of Kyoto, Nara and other important cultural centres (monthly programmes are detailed in a quarterly newsletter available at the TIC or directly from the museum).

Although it's not possible to say with certainty what you can see at any one time, the most important works are practically always on display. They include rare 7th- and 8th-century Buddhist painting and sculpture, both small-scale and monumental, as well as the brilliantly coloured and vividly dramatic narrative scrolls of the Heian (10th to 12th centuries) and Ka-

---

Odd Little Symbol

On your guide maps to Kyoto, you'll notice, perhaps with an uneasy start, that the temples are indicated with a swastika, albeit with the bars on the cross pointing in an unfamiliar direction. In fact, you'll see the swastika everywhere in Buddhist sculpture and architecture, marking the breast of statues or even on the cups of holy water you're offered before starting your climb of Mt. Fuji. The Japanese call this symbol manji and take its four bars to symbolize the Four Great Truths of Buddhism.

Although the sign appeared all over the world in ancient times —China, Egypt, Greece, Persia, Scotland, Ireland and even South and Central America—one of its earliest forms is believed to have originated in India, where the Sanskrit word swastika means "good luck". It is thought to have crossed the Himalayas on its way to Japan with the spread of Buddhism, though it is by no means an exclusively Buddhist symbol (early Christianity put it on pulpits, tombs and church bells).

It was only in 1919 when Hitler reversed the swastika's bars in a clockwise form that the sign took on its notorious significance as the symbol of the Nazi Party. The Japanese could have told Hitler—not that it would have worried him—that the clockwise form had the unlucky significance of "away from God". Meanwhile, as H. G. Wells said in his Outline of World History, "This odd little symbol spins gaily around the world".

makura (13th century) periods. Look out for the landscapes of the great 15th-century Muromachi painter Sesshu and the delicate birds and flowers painted by his contemporary, Shokei. The museum also has fine exhibits of weapons, traditional armour developed by the Kamakura warlords, and ten centuries of costume, including some dazzling examples, with masks, from the *noh* theatre.

Archery contests on horseback are a major attraction at festivals.

The archaeological department displays pottery and artefacts from the prehistoric Jomon and Yayoi periods and an important collection of Chinese ceramics ranging from the Stone Age to the Ming dynasty.

South of the National Museum, right across the street, is the spectacular **Sanjusangendo**, literally the "Hall of Thirty-Three Bays" (between the pillars supporting the 387-foot [118-m.]-long building). The original temple of 1164 survived only 100 years, but its 13th-century reconstruction is what you see today, intact. Its centrepiece is an 11-foot (3.3-m.)-high gilded seated wooden statue of the Kannon Bodhisattva with 11 faces on the crown of its head and "a thousand arms"—actually only 40, wielding bells, wheels and lotus flowers, but each, says the doctrine, endowed with the power to save 25 worlds. The astounding spectacle of Sanjusangendo, however, is created by the grandiose army of 1,000 other gilded images of the Kannon—truly 1,000, count them—standing at prayerful attention all around the central figure in perfect formation. When you've recovered from the massive overall impact, admire the dignity of the individual statues, even though they are identical, carved by the 13th-century masters Kokei, Unkei and his son Tankei (creator of the central Kannon at the age of 82), with 70 assistants.

Behind these massed Buddhas is a corridor with another 28 superb statues of the ferocious Gods of Wind (Fujin) and Thunder (Raijin), along with attendant spirits of variously grim, forbidding or serene demeanour to exorcize evil or protect the worthy. The carvings here are as intensely personal as the 1,001 Buddhas are uniform, the undoubted masterpiece being a gaunt hermit in rags, Basusennin. The long straight corridor itself has served since the 17th century as an archery range, and a *toshiya* archery contest is still held here every January.

Fire was less kind to the nearby **Chishakuin Temple** in 1947, destroying some priceless old painted screens, but 16th-century tea master Senno Rikyu's beautiful garden makes a good resting-place if you have a bad case of "sightseeing feet".

Ukyo and Kita

These wards, to give them their proper municipal name, on the west and north sides of Kyoto, include the bulk of the city's most important temples amid the beautiful countryside of gentle hills and forest that prompted the emperor's spiritual advisers to choose this site for his capital. We give just a few representative temples, both for their important art treasures and their lovely gardens. Some are monumental, others small and intimate. Others still you'll discover for yourself as you wander from place to place. Plan your tour, by taxi or on foot from bus or train, with map in hand, to "do" just two or three temples in a morning.

Ryoanji (59 bus to Ryoanjimae stop or Kitano Line on the Keifuku railway to Ryoanji-michi Station). Standing at the northwest corner of Kyoto, this is without a doubt the most famous of all Zen Buddhist temples. Its garden has provoked more words of debate, both admiring and derogatory, than you could count chips of white gravel in its rectangular 98 by 32 feet (30 by 10 m.): no trees, no shrubs, just 15 grey rocks with a little green moss at their base standing in groups of five, three, two, three and two amid the carefully raked white gravel. Opposite the wooden verandah from which you contemplate the garden, a wall of brown clay runs the length and far side of the garden. Over the 500 years since the garden was laid out, the oil in which the clay was boiled has seeped through to

create a wonderful undulating pattern of light and dark.

The total effect of the garden is awesomely simple. It is perhaps the essence of Zen Buddhism's profoundly anti-intellectual teachings that the garden defies definition. People see dark islands in a white sea, or mountain peaks above the clouds. People see what they want to see. Ryoanji's abbot, Genryu Kino-shita, has suggested that, in addition to its traditional name of Seki-tei ("Garden of Stones"), it might better be known as Mu-tei ("Garden of Nothingness") or Ru-tei ("Garden of Emptiness"). In view of the garden's ineffable mystery, it's appro-

The Golden Pavilion, a luxurious hideaway from worldly cares.

priate that, although the "landscaping" is usually attributed to the great master Soami, nobody knows for sure who really created it.

Once again, it's best to get there very early in the morning before the crowds arrive. Ryoanji's beauty is such that it impels respect from most onlookers, but even if it doesn't, you can quickly forget the others and lose or find yourself in that sea—sky?—nothingness?—and for a magic moment create your own world.

Don't ignore the rest of the temple grounds. Beyond the rock garden you can walk among the maples and pines of the forest surrounding the lovely Kyoyochi Pond at the foot of Mt. Kinugasa.

Kinkakuji (59 or 204 bus to Kinkakuji-michi stop) is famous for quite another reason. Of all the Japanese monuments to have burned down in the past 2,000 years, none has been so celebrated for its fire as this "Temple of the Golden Pavilion", subject of one of Yukio Mishima's most popular novels. Architecturally, the original 14th-century pavilion, completely covered in gold leaf, was typical of the Muromachi style's aesthetic opulence favoured by Shogun Yoshimitsu Ashikaga, who built it as a hideaway from his worldly worries. A young Buddhist monk angrily burned it down in 1950. According to Mishima, the monk resented the self-indulgent life spent there by his superior, no doubt inspired by the ancient shogun's own ambivalent attitude to self-denial in such luxurious surroundings. Appropriately, a bronze phoenix today perches on top of the reconstructed three-storey pavilion, in style a bizarre mixture of a Heian palace, Kamakura samurai villa and Zen temple, projecting out over a large pond. An interesting antithesis to Ryoanji.

Daitokuji Temple (206 loop bus to Daitokuji-mae stop) is in fact a Chinese-style complex of temples and 22 affiliated monasteries built and rebuilt from the 14th to 17th centuries. It's certainly the most richly endowed in artistic treasures and gardens in the city. You can spend a whole morning or afternoon wandering from one little temple to another, each with its own individual character.

Be sure to see the **Daisen-in**, "Zen Temple Without Equal", at the north end of the compound. The great Kano clan of 16th-century artists, led here by Motonobu and Yukinobu, have left some splendid painted *fusuma* (sliding panels) depicting monks at study, a motif of birds and flowers, and the changing seasons. The gardens of the Daisen-in subtly vary richness and simplicity, some with rocks and gravel, raked flat or in mounds, others with waterfalls, trees, shrubs and moss. Symbolism abounds—a turtle island for the material life, a crane island for spirituality, a footstep of Buddha, a bridge of youth, and once again you add your personal interpretation from your own meditations.

At the **Juko-in** monastery west of Daisen-in is the cemetery where the most celebrated of all tea masters, Senno-Rikyu, is buried. His death in 1591 by *seppuku* (the ritual disembowelling more crudely known to Westerners as *harakiri*, "belly-slitting") is said to have been preceded by one last meticulous tea ceremony in his favourite pavilion.

In the south-west corner of the compound, at the end of the path leading from the main entrance, **Zuiho-in** is a curiosity notable for its gardens' combination of Zen Buddhism and Christianity. The monastery was founded in 1546 by Sorin Ohtomo, a warlord of Zen persuasion who was converted several years later to Christianity by a Jesuit priest and christened Francisco. He continued bloody campaigns against rival Buddhist monasteries, calling them "crusades". Francisco Sorin Ohtomo is best known for sending a mission to Rome, Japan's first diplomatic emissaries to Europe.

Two of the monastery gardens have been laid out in classical Zen style, with rocks, mosses and raked white gravel, but are said to incorporate Christian motifs. The north garden is known as the Garden of the Cross, its rocks rather fancifully said to allude to the crucifix. The South Garden, with its rocks built up onto a mound of moss and shrubs, is known as the **Zuiho-tei** ("Garden of the Blissful Mountain") believed by Christians to symbolize Jesus's Sermon on the Mount. The Buddhist abbot of the monastery declares it to represent "the dauntless, unshakable mind of a Bodhisattva full of compassion". But you may like best of all the lovely smooth pavingstone garden of the Asho-ken teahouse west of the priests' quarters, with no apparent symbolism at all.

Koryuji Temple (Keifuku-Arashiyama Line to Uzumasa Station) is of historical importance as the temple dedicated to 7th-century Prince Shotoku, revered as one of the nation's earliest great lawgivers (see p. 23). A statue of the prince, who was also known as Taishi, popularly believed to have been carved by the prince's own hand, is shown like a religious relic only once a year, November 22, in the temple's Taishido Hall.

The Lecture Hall (dating from 1165) is the oldest surviving

wooden structure in Kyoto and houses three statues from the 8th and 9th centuries. But the main interest of Koryuji is its modern **Reihokan Museum,** boasting a superb collection of medieval sculptures. The most famous is the charming Miroku Bosatsu (Bodhisattva) from the 7th century, seated in what looks like a very casual but in fact spiritually formal *hankashii* meditation pose, with the right foot crossed over the left thigh, the right elbow leaning on the knee and the right hand delicately poised. The smile is as enigmatic as any Leonardo da Vinci ever imagined. There are also ten fine temple guardian statues from the 11th-century Heian period and a lovely Kisshoten Goddess of Fortune.

As you walk north of the Koryuji Temple along lanes of bamboo groves, look out for the occasional glimpse of beautiful private gardens tended with as much meticulous care as those of the temples.

Whatever discoveries you may make for yourself in Ukyo, you may also pass the **Nembutsuji Temple**, with its 8,000 small stone Buddhas that served as tombstones for the anonymous poor from the Ada-shino neighbourhood from the 9th to the 19th centuries; or the **Seiryoji Temple**, with a wonderful mountain backdrop; or the **Tenryuji Temple** popular with elderly

gentlemen for its *go* club just inside the entrance, and with their wives who like the Sogenchi goldfish pond and the garden of maples and japonica gently climbing the hillside; or the **Saihoji Temple** famous for its "strolling" garden with an enchanting variety of greens and yellows in its 40-odd species of moss, so that the place is also known as Kokedera ("Moss Temple").

Central Kyoto

The area immediately north of Kyoto Station, brings together the city ancient and modern. The skyline is dominated by the red and white candle-like "space needle", **Kyoto Tower**, looming over high-rise hotels and department stores. Beyond the tower are the headquarters of two schools of the "Pure Land" Jodo-Shinshu sect, the Nishi-Honganji and Higashi-Honganji

Zuiho-in's Zen rock-garden has a new meaning for each visitor.

temples. The latter was built by Shogun Ieyasu Tokugawa to split and counteract the menacingly powerful influence of Nishi-Honganji, which had won thousands of followers with its free-wheeling Buddhism allowing priests to marry and have children, permit-

119

ting meat-eating and renouncing traditional ascetic practices.

The **Nishi-Honganji**, just a ten-minute walk north-west of Kyoto Station, is the classical example of monumental Japanese Buddhist architecture combining a bold, dramatic silhouette with lavish ornamentation. The 17th-century buildings owe much of their splendour to the structures brought here from Hideyoshi's opulent Fushimi Castle on the south side of Kyoto (dismantled lock, stock and barrel by a Tokugawa in 1632).

The great **Daishoin Hall** with its Chinese-style Shikyakumon Gate, beautifully carved by Jingoro "Left-Handed" Hidari, came from the old castle. The paintings on the interior wall panels, ceilings and sliding screens are by the greatest artists of the Kano school. The abbot chose as his audience room the richly decorated Ko-no-Ma ("Stork Chamber") which Hideyoshi had used for his council hall. Be sure to see the wild geese exquisitely carved by Hidari on the wooden transom.

In the south-east corner of the temple grounds, the three-storey **Hiunkaku Pavilion** is a lovely example of the much simpler quarters which Hideyoshi used for his private purposes (brought here from his Jurakudai Mansion). The bathroom, bedroom and tea salon, again with some superb Kano paintings, are lovingly preserved.

A **Costume Museum**, tracing the history of Japanese clothes, is located in Horikawa Street, opposite the temple.

Most of **Higashi-Honganji** is closed to the public, but the Main Hall and Founder's Hall, rebuilt in 1895 after repeated fires, are notable for the 50 ropes of human hair still on display after being donated by women worshippers to haul the temple's pillars into position.

Nijo Castle (9 or 52 bus to Nijojo-mae stop) is a poignant monument to the ironic twists of history. It was built by Ieyasu Tokugawa in 1603 for his occasional, reluctant visits to Kyoto. The castle was taken over by the Emperor Meiji at the time of the Restoration. It was here that the emperor signed the edict which abolished the shogunate and sent his carpenters round the castle to replace the Tokugawa hollyhock crest with the imperial chrysanthemum. In some of the more inaccessible parts of the woodwork you can still make out one or two recalcitrant hollyhocks. The grounds have all the moat, ramparts and turrets of a castle, but the central buildings of the Ninomaru Palace look more like the attractive country residence of a ruler who does not really fear siege or attack. Costumed models of the shogun and his feudal lords can be seen in the grand Audience Chamber. Outside his room, the shogun had a "nightingale floor" installed, with planks specially constructed to squeak with the warble of a nightingale if anybody was approaching along the corridor.

These jars of sake are intended for holy offerings at the temple.

The trees you see in the gardens were all planted after the Meiji Restoration. It is said that Tokugawa preferred his gardens without trees because he didn't want his warriors depressed by the melancholy contemplation of falling leaves in autumn.

Just south of Nijo Castle is the remnant of the historic **Shinsen-en Garden**, part of the grand 10th-century Heian palace built

at the time of Kyoto's foundation. In its carefully restored Chinese-style landscaping around a central pond, you may imagine the boating parties and poetry recitals that once took place here.

For a change of pace and mood, seek out **Nishiki Market**, (Nishiki-koji Dori one block north of the main department stores). This remarkably tranquil street market is housed under one arcade. There's pure art to be seen in the colourful stands of dried fish, fresh fish, wonderfully arranged pickles, stout young bamboo shoots, chickens neatly carved into wings and breasts and then arranged in elaborate patterns, and a whole cornucopia of squid, mussels, oysters and giant scallops. All very busy, but with the peaceful essence of Japanese form and order, as much Kyoto as any temple garden.

Environs of Kyoto

When you want a little break from sightseeing there's the Hozu River (or Oi as it's also known hereabouts) in the resort area of **Arashiyama**. From the Togetsukyo Bridge, you can take a rowing boat or a green-roofed *yakata* boat, once used for fishing and aristocratic cruises, punted along by bamboo pole for a view of Mt. Ogura. With luck, a ''picnic-boat'' may pull alongside to serve you *sushi*

snacks or *tempura* cooked fresh and hot right there on the boat.

If you're feeling more adventurous, plan to shoot the **Hozu Rapids**. Take the JR train on the San-In Line from Kyoto Station to Kameoka and walk about eight minutes to the boathouse at Hozu Bridge. The boat brings you to Arashiyama and you can start your temple tour from there. Flat-bottomed boats holding up to 20 people are steered with oar and bamboo pole by the crew of three men, and the roaring Hozu does the rest. The 10-mile (16-km.) run lasts about 90 minutes. It's thrilling, but not at all dangerous. Take something waterproof. Sheer rock face and dense forest come right down to the water's edge. Another antithesis to the Ryoanji rock garden.

Nara

The town of Nara owes its existence to that moment at the beginning of the 8th century when the Japanese nation had to start organizing itself as a political reality. There were taxes to levy, law and order to be imposed, provinces to be administered, all that through a government with an emperor in some kind of permanent headquarters, the country's first settled imperial capital—Nara. In less complicated times, up to the year 710, the seat of government had moved from place to place with the advent of each new emperor. It was in fact an empress, feisty 50-year-old Gemmyo, who put a stop to these imperial wanderings and settled down in Nara, situated in a shallow basin of the Yamato plain, protected to the east by a crescent of wooded hills.

The 74 years known as the Nara period saw the first great flowering of Buddhism as a national religion, and Japanese architects and sculptors began developing a national style in the new capital's temples and Buddhist statuary, moving slowly away from their earlier, purely Chinese inspiration. It was here that the spirit of Japanese culture was forged and given its first distinctive form. Clan rivalries for control of the imperial throne brought Nara's sweet moment in the sun to an end and the capital was moved to Kyoto. But Nara's spiritual and cultural legacy has endured. For centuries the town remained a quiet country backwater, overshadowed by the thrust of Osaka and the brilliance of Kyoto, but always venerated as the place where the Japanese seek out the beginnings of their civilization. It deserves a pilgrimage by anyone really wanting to know Japan.

The JR train takes just over an hour from Kyoto, so you may prefer the 33-minute trip with the Kinki Nippon Railway. Most of the sights of Nara are within the city limits and can be comfortably visited on a one-day excursion. But there are also, just outside the city, some truly important temples—the Toshodaiji, Yakushiji and, above all, the Horyuji, considered one of the two or three most significant monuments in the country. If you get to Nara very early in the morning and head straight out to Horyuji and its nearby temples *before* visiting Nara proper in the afternoon, you could fit everything into one day. However, to do it all more leisurely justice, plan on an overnight stay.

Like any place of pilgrimage anywhere in the world, Nara doesn't escape its dose of commercialized crudity, and the souvenirs, trinkets and junk food seem a little more tawdry than usual. But you can quickly leave all that behind you as you discover the real beauties and pleasures of the ancient capital.

The historic area of the city is on the east side of the modern town at the end of the main street, Sanjo-dori. The temples, shrines and museum are nearly all encompassed by **Nara Park**, largest of its kind in the country. The park's most conspicuous residents are 1,000 wild but very tame deer, regarded as "divine messengers" and so not hunted, though the antlers procured from natural deaths are much valued for the souvenir trade. At sunset, you can hear a trumpeter calling the little beasts home to their pens.

Start over on the west side of the park at **Todaiji Temple**, entrance through the great Nandaimon Gate. The gate's wooden Deva King statues are splendid 13th-century works by Unkei and his son Tankei. The temple is a sanctuary of superlatives, housing the world's largest bronze statue in the world's largest wooden structure, the **Daibutsuden**, Hall of the Great Buddha. Before you go in, take a good look at the particularly fine 8th-century octagonal bronze lantern in front, with its eight Buddha figures playing musical instruments.

The hall is ritually protected

against fire by the two great Chinese *shibi* (tails of the *shi* bird) at either end of its roof ridge, but in this case it didn't help much. The Great Buddha—**Daibutsu**—was completed in the year 752, but civil war, two fires and two earthquakes have destroyed the hall and systematically attacked head, limbs and torso of the statue until very little of the original casting still

stands. Some of the clothing and lotus petals at the base are authenticated as parts of the 8th-century work, but everything else has had to be painstakingly re-modelled for it still to weigh in at its original 437 tons. (Notice, for instance, how much darker the head is than the rest of the body.) Some other futile but fascinating statistics of gigantism: the statue is 53 feet (16.2 m.) high with eyes 3 feet 9 inches (1.2 m.) wide and thumbs 5 feet (1.6 m.) long. Or, put another way, the left hand is big enough to hold a sumo wrestling ring and, during the annual cleaning in August, workers in white kimonos can be seen crawling in one nostril and out the other.

The Daibutsu is revered by the Todaiji's Kegon sect as representing the Birushana-Butsu or Buddha Vairocana, the very root or source of Buddha's essence. Best viewed from the left-hand side, he sits cross-legged on a 56-petal lotus pedestal in a posture of preaching, offering peace of mind with his right hand and the fulfilment of the faithfuls' wishes with his left. He is benignly flanked in front by two handsome late 17th-century gilded wooden Buddha figures and protected in the rear by two

Ancient Bugaku *dance drama is still performed today.*

Heavenly Guardians, Komokuten (left) and Tamonten (right), both busily trampling demons and frightening away any other evil spirits attempting to approach.

Next to the Komokuten, on the right, is an interesting model of the complete Todaiji temple compound as it was first conceived, including at the time two seven-storey pagodas. The huge Nandaimon Gate was then exactly two-thirds the size of the great hall, which has been reduced in repeated reconstructions to 60 per cent of its original size—still the world's biggest—but today the proportions are lost.

Not all is so solemn back there behind the Buddha. There's also a pillar with a hole chiselled out at the base; if you can wriggle through it, you're guaranteed a place in heaven and the enthusiastic applause of all onlookers.

On a little hill east of the Todaiji are two satellite temples, the Nigatsudo (February Hall) and **Sangatsudo** (March Hall). The latter, also known as Hokkedo, is open to the public and has an intriguing gilded statue of an eight-armed Buddha with snares and ropes to catch sinners, but also with a poignant expression of compassion.

If you have plenty of time to stroll, **Wakakusayama Hill** offers some lovely walks south to the cedar forest on Mt. Kasuga with **Kasuga Shrine** at the foot.

Wandering in this green and pleasant setting, you'll find sightseeing becomes almost incidental. The avenue leading to this Shinto shrine of the ancient Fujiwara clan is bordered by some 3,000 stone and bronze lanterns donated by family members and feudal vassals. The shrine itself is of classical Shinto simplicity: it used to be dismantled and renewed every 20 years, but the custom seems to have been discontinued.

In the centre of the park is **Nara National Museum**, one of the country's most important repositories of national art treasures. Like Kyoto's museum, it presents rotating exhibitions of sculpture and painting on loan from surrounding temples. It's often the best way to see these works—well lit and better displayed than in the temples' treasure houses, and without such big crowds. A particularly appealing part of the museum's permanent collection is the portrait of the temples' priests, showing a few of them to be more cynically worldly than their followers might have imagined.

Back at the western end of the park is the **Kofukuji Temple**, symbolized by its five-storey pagoda at the edge of Sarusawa

The Heavenly Guardian keeps evil away from the Daibutsu at Nara.

Pond, perhaps the most commonly photographed image of Nara itself.

Kofukuji was the Fujiwara clan's private Buddhist temple transferred from Umasaka to Nara in 710, Buddhism and Shinto then going very much hand in hand in any family with political as well as spiritual aspirations. The Buddhist monks later came in handy as warriors in the Fujiwara wars against the Taira clan, who burned down both Kofukuji and Todaiji. The Kofukuji pagoda was rebuilt in 1426.

Just north of the pagoda is the temple's **Kokuhokan Treasure House**, the most prized exhibit being an 8th-century drylacquer sculpture of the guardian deity, Asura. In addition, there is a splendid 17th-century bronze Yakushi Nyorai (Buddha of Healing) and an early Nara-period group of eight Buddha-messengers, as well as Unkei's celebrated 16th-century statues of two Buddhist sages, Muchaku and Seshin.

From the city's eastern hills, you may catch a glimpse of one of the ancient imperial capital's most incongruous attractions— **Nara Dreamland**. Yes, this is a Japanese version of America's Disneyland, complete with Yesterdayland, Tomorrowland and a host of other rather uninspired fantasies. If you're stuck with some kids who just can't stand any more temples, let them ride Dreamland's 2-mile (3-km.) miniature railway (20-minute bus ride from Nara Station).

To visit the three major temples on the south-west outskirts of Nara—Toshodaiji, Yakushiji and Horyuji—it's ideally worth hiring a taxi for half a day, but they can also be visited by bus on a 110-minute round trip from Kintetsu-Nara Station (with some short walks in between).

Toshodaiji Temple is a noble 8th-century edifice founded by the heroic Chinese monk Chien Chen, known to the Japanese as Ganjin. He brought to Japan the strict ascetic principles of Chinese Buddhism only after five unsuccessful attempts to cross the Sea of Japan to Honshu island over a period of 12 years. He finally arrived completely blind but still able to preach the precepts of his faith and ordain an abdicated emperor and empress.

It is felt that Ganjin's purity of purpose finds supreme expression in the great simplicity of Toshodaiji's architecture, especially the Kondo, Main Hall. The Japanese like to compare its slightly curving pillars, in architectural principle at least, to those of the Greek Parthenon.

Ganjin's tomb is in the northeast corner of the temple grounds, a simple monument in a quiet little garden beyond a crescent-shaped pond. West of his tomb is the Mieido (Founder's Hall) in which Ganjin's seated statue, said to be carved as he was about to die, is exhibited only once a year, June 6, on the anniversary of his death in 763.

The temple's Treasure House is interesting as an example of Azekura construction, that is, cypress beams without nails which contract in the dry season to allow air to circulate, and expand in the wet season to absorb humidity and keep out the cold.

A ten-minute walk due south leads you directly to **Yakushiji Temple**, originally founded in 680, though the buildings you will see are almost all date from the 13th century and later. The one wonderful survivor of the pre-Nara period is the ethereally graceful three-storey East Pagoda erected in 698. At first sight it appears to have six storeys, because of additional roofs—*mokoshi*—inserted beneath each principal roof. (The pagoda in Japanese temple-doctrine is regarded as having originally been a mausoleum for the Buddha, with many of the most important said to contain some of his ashes in the uppermost of the two bowls set in the *suien* or spire at the top of the pagoda. The second bowl contains the holy *sutras*—Buddhist scriptures.)

The temple's most cherished treasure is the black bronze Ya-

kushi Triad in the **Kondo** Main Hall. These 7th-century statues of the Buddha of Healing flanked by attendants Nikko (Sunlight) and Gakko (Moonlight) are marvels of delicately expressive line and form. The sophisticated sculpture of the silk draping, necklaces and vines and the figures of tortoise, dragon, white tiger and phoenix around the pedestals are all testimony to influences from Greece, Persia, India and China—the route of the Silk Road between Europe and Asia.

Horyuji Temple, 7 miles (11 km.) west of town, is the jewel of Nara's monumental temples. Japan's oldest existing temple, it comprises 36 buildings, many of them among the world's oldest wooden structures. Together, they offer one of the most beautiful collections of architecture, sculpture and painting in the country.

You enter the **Saiin** (Western Temple) by the great southern Nandaimon Gate, rebuilt in the 15th century, and walk along the 1,400-year-old avenue to the Chumon Gate, erected in the year of the temple's foundation by Prince Shotoku in 607. The gateway is divided by pillars into two entrances, originally one for the prince and one for his revered aunt, Empress Suiko. The Deva Kings, one scarlet for the spirits of light and one black for

Horyuji Temple was central to the foundation of Japanese Buddhism.

the spirits of darkness, were carved 100 years later.

In the courtyard to the right of the Chumon stands the **Kondo** Main Hall displaying a superb bronze Sakyamuni or historical embodiment of the Buddha, Gautama, dated 623, with four fine and sturdy Heavenly Guard-ians. The five-storey **pagoda** is also one of the first buildings dating from the temple's foundation. Dismantled before the outbreak of World War II, the original timbers of 607 were reassembled. When the central pillar of the pagoda was taken down, a bronze vase was discovered at the base, itself containing a silver vase enclosing a third vase, of glass, holding what are believed to be bones of the

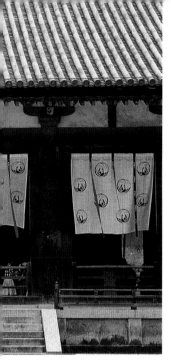

great wooden Kudara Kannon, a graceful figure standing 7 feet (2.1 m.) high, believed to be the work of a Korean artist, and the Tamamushi Shrine depicting on its walls and door paintings of scenes from the life of the Buddha—both from the 7th century. You can also see statues of Prince Shotoku dating from the 10th and 13th centuries. The prince is one of the most frequently portrayed figures of Japanese history.

In the Toin or East Temple, you'll find the beautiful octagonal **Yumedono** (Hall of Dreams) where Prince Shotoku went to study the Buddhist scriptures and claimed to have received assistance from an ancient sage who appeared to him in a vision whenever he was stumped by an obscure passage in the *sutra*. The hall displays several fine wooden Buddha figures of the early Nara period.

One last building to visit in the Horyuji precincts is the tranquil **Chuguji** nunnery. There's a charming, beatific Miroku Bosatsu, popularly believed to be the work of Prince Shotoku and comparable to its counterpart in the Koryuji Treasure House in Kyoto. But the most prized art work here is the oldest existing fragment of Japanese embroidery, the early 7th-century Tenjukoku *Mandara*, "Land of Heavenly Longevity".

Buddha. (The relic is not usually displayed.)

The Kondo directly beyond the pagoda is worth a visit for its model of the original 7th-century layout of Horyuji.

Immediately to the east of the Saiin complex is the important **Daihozoden** (Great Treasure Hall), a modern 20th-century building housing the temple's most delicate and most ancient masterpieces. They include the

Osaka

If your flight to Japan continues on to Osaka from Tokyo, you will find that the town makes a very convenient base for your visits to Kyoto (50 minutes by local train) and Nara (31 minutes). It also gives you a good excuse for taking a look round this astonishing city. Most people feel they do need an excuse, because Osaka itself is such a single-mindedly commercial and industrial centre that it has left little thought to seducing visitors with urban beautification. People complain of pollution, general industrial blight and a brash and bumptious population obsessed by worship of the almighty yen. Nonetheless, there *are* things to be seen here, a couple of really good museums and, not least, some underground shopping cities that dwarf anything even Tokyo has to offer. It's also a very appropriate place to take an Industrial Tour, if you're not planning one in Tokyo (see p. 75).

In any case, you may well feel it's worth at least one day of your time to put your finger on the pulse of that national economic dynamo right here in this perpetual boomtown. (Osaka has recently been ousted by Yokohama from its number two position in population size, but in every other respect—above all, revenue and sheer physical size—Osaka bows only to Tokyo, and that very reluctantly.)

There was a time when Osaka was in a slump. That was back in the 4th century when, noticing that the village fires were burning low, Emperor Nintoku offered to suspend taxes for three years. The place brightened up and, 1,600 years later, the village fires burn high, as you can see from the chimney stacks of Osaka's 30,000 factories—steel, chemicals, textiles, printing and food processing. And the revenue from the taxes of the mammoth wholesale merchandising companies—Osaka is *the* distribution centre for Japanese products—must be too nice for the government ever to think of suspending them again.

It was Hideyoshi who really exploited the gold mine of the Osakans' business acumen for the national treasury by building his gigantic castle here in the 16th century and offering special business incentives for commercial investment. The Tokugawas destroyed the castle, but not Osaka's earning ability. World War II bombs devastated three quarters of the city, but it rebuilt fast, bigger than ever. Fittingly, Osaka staged the world Expo 70 fair, to symbolize Japan's economic recovery, and the place where all the Japanese banknotes and coins are manufactured is located right here, too.

Not that Osaka is nothing but money, money, money. For centuries it was also the centre of Japan's theatrical culture, producing in Monzaemon Chikamatsu (1653–1724) a playwright the Japanese like to compare to Shakespeare. At any rate, his heroic and tragic dramas make stirring fare for Osaka's own unique contribution to national drama still going strong in its old Dotombori theatre district: the *bunraku* puppet theatre for adults (see p.195). And like Lyons in France, Osaka is a business town which its demanding merchants have made a gastronomic heaven. Osaka's cuisine is considered the most inventive and tasty—but not the cheapest—in the country.

Touring Osaka is best done by taxi or subway (the bus stops are practically all indicated in Japanese characters only). Osaka Station and its adjoining subway, Umeda, are the best places to begin your visit (Osaka City Tourist Information Office is right by the main station.) The business and entertainment district, popularly known as **Kita**, is the very essence of modern Osaka bustle. You'll find the major office skyscrapers and cinemas here, as well as the gigantic Hankyu and Hanshin department stores (which also run private railways to Kyoto and Kobe). At rush hour, Umeda's teeming subway platforms rival anything you may see at Tokyo's Shinjuku. The underground city at Umeda is a mammoth non-stop operation of shops, bars and restaurants that is both commercially deadly serious and somehow exhilaratingly cheerful.

The **Mint** is situated on the west bank of the Yodo River (opposite Sakuranomiya Park). Its museum has a large and fascinating exhibition of the history of Japanese and foreign money, but if you are interested in seeing the modern stuff being made, you have to book a visit ten days in advance.

Just east of Sakuranomiya Park is the **Fujita Art Museum**, with a great collection of Chinese and Japanese paintings from the 11th century to the present day. If you have become an adept of the tea ceremony, you'll especially appreciate the excellent collection of 14th-century ceramics—tea bowls, tea kettles and caddies, as well as bamboo spoons, whisks and flower vases.

Nakanoshima is an island in the middle of the Yodo River with most of Osaka's municipal buildings on it, including a European-style town hall. But, more importantly for the foreign visitor, there's a park at the eastern end with an ideal pho-

Nightlife in Osaka is as bright and bouncy as a pachinko *pinball.*

tographic view of Hideyoshi's **Osaka Castle** (illuminated at night). You may be content just to photograph it, because the castle has been destroyed and rebuilt so many times that today it is little more than a grandiose urban symbol. To celebrate his unification of Japan after more than a century of civil war, Hideyoshi had made it the country's greatest fortress, so the Tokugawas felt obliged to destroy it in 1615 after snatching power away from Hideyoshi's heir. They later rebuilt it to bolster their own prestige and burned it down again in chagrin when their shogunate came to an end in 1868.

Today, a reinforced concrete

134

replica offers just the great 138-
foot (42-m.)-high, five-storied
dungeon tower, surrounded by
moat and ramparts, the latter
nicely ivy-covered now for a
picturesque antique touch. The
castle honours the memory of
Hideyoshi with a **museum** housing armour, weapons, period costumes and historical documents
of his times. There's also an enchanting collection of *bunraku*
puppets.

With a welcome touch of green
amid all the asphalt, gingko and
plane trees line the attractive **Midosuji Boulevard** running down
to Kita's southern counterpart,
Minami, around Shinsaibashi
Station. This shopping centre
aims at a more traditional "old
Osaka" atmosphere, with old-
fashioned little shops, *Osaka-
zushi* (don't say *sushi* here) and

135

charming taverns. Some rather original lighting gives Minami's underground area its name Niji-no-machi, "Rainbow City".

Further south, near Ebisucho Station, you can get a panoramic view of the city with an elevator-ride to the observation deck of 338-foot (103-m.)-high **Tsuten-kaku Tower** (every city's apparently obligatory communications tower).

The **Osaka Municipal Art Museum** (Tennoji Station) is worth a visit for the celebrated Abe Collection of 200 Chinese paintings from the 9th to the 13th centuries, as well as its Ming- and Ching-dynasty ceramics (14th to 19th centuries).

The **Dotombori** theatre district (Nipponbashi Station), where you can see the country's only authentic *bunraku* performances at the Asahiza Theatre, is also the location of the city's best restaurants. In the view of many gourmets, that means the best in the whole country.

The Shin-Kabukiza Theatre on Midosuji Boulevard in fact gives *kabuki* performances only three weeks in the year, but there's plenty of other traditional drama such as *kyogen* farces and *manzai* comic dialogue. The springtime Osaka International Festival of drama and music takes place here, as well as at the Festival Hall on Nakanoshima Island.

Kobe

Hemmed into a narrow coastal strip between the Rokko Mountains and the Inland Sea, this port-town, like Yokohama, came into its own after American pressure opened Japan up to foreign trade in the 1860s. Today it derives its cosmopolitan atmosphere from the considerable foreign business community still residing here.

Since it is also a port of call for luxury cruise-liners, you may be lucky enough to have your first view of Kobe from its **harbour**, completely modernized since its total destruction in World War II. For an impressive view of the harbour facilities, the 356-foot (108-m.)-high **Port Tower** on Naka Pier has a panoramic observation deck. If you've not come in by ship yourself, take the 50-minute **port cruise** starting from Naka Pier.

One of the other important effects of Kobe's foreign residents is the development of the now nationally famous Kobe beef in a country that, until these foreigners began demanding steaks, never touched the stuff. Raised in nearby Tajima or Tamba, the beef, carefully butchered and aged in Kobe, owes its special flavour in part to the cattle's daily tipple of strong beer. The price in the restaurants on Tor Road is exorbitant, but you might like to try the beef either grilled

Chubby-cheeked wood-carvings make good souvenirs.

straight or prepared Japanese-style as *sashimi* (raw), *sukiyaki* (thinly sliced and pan-fried) or *shabu-shabu* (stewed in a soup).

The city's two big downtown shopping centres, both with large department stores and elegant fashion boutiques, are Sanno-miya and Motomachi. You'll find some quaint smaller shops on the arcaded Kokashita Sho-ten-gai under the JR elevated railway.

In the old foreign residential neighbourhood of **Kitano**, you can see some of the 19th-century European-style houses that survived the war—they are great curiosities for Japanese tourists.

Kobe is also especially appreciated for its *sake*, and the **Hakutsuru Sake Brewery Museum** shows the lovely old tools and utensils they used to use before everything was streamlined in plastic and stainless steel.

One other attraction is Kobe's transport innovation, *Portliner*, a driverless computerized train linking Port Island out in the harbour with the district of Sannomiya.

ᨀ Ise-Shima

Ise-Shima National Park, southeast of Osaka, is the sacred repository of the national identity, the seat of the country's two most venerable Shinto sanctuaries dedicated nearly 2,000 years ago to Japan's founding deities. Here, among simple modest edifices erected in the serenest of wooded landscapes, you will get a keener sense than at any other shrine of the Japanese people's reverential attachment to their country and its mythic origins.

While neither more nor less profound than the sentiments of Americans for their White House and the Declaration of Independence, of the British for the Houses of Parliament and the Magna Carta or of the French for the Bastille and the ideals of Liberty, Equality and Fraternity, the Japanese national pride embodied in the shrines of Ise-Shima is quite detached from man-made institutions. What is paramount at Ise-Shima, as can be seen in the carefully orchestrated approach to the sanctuaries past the limpid Isuzu River and through the forest, is nature itself. The buildings are sacred indeed as focuses for a moment of worship of the national *idea*, but they are dismantled and renewed every 20 years, as fresh as the new generations of pilgrims who come to visit them. The national identity, the solidarity with the ancestral deities of the imperial family, endures in the whole setting of Ise-Shima.

It is to Ise-Shima that the emperor has always gone to worship at important moments of national history, an imperial marriage or birth, an enthronement or a crisis of war or natural catastrophe. And millions of ordinary citizens still go there annually to pay homage. To join them is to get closer to an understanding of Japan's mystique.

If you're going there directly, the shrines are most conveniently reached from Nagoya by the Kinki-Nippon Railway to Uji-Yamada Station. But you may prefer to explore more of the peninsula, its national park and the resort town of Kashikojima, southern terminus of the Kinki-Nippon's Shima line. At the shrines themselves, buses take you from one to the other.

Geku, the Outer Shrine, just a

short walk from Uji-Yamada Station, is dedicated to the God of the Earth, sent down to Japan by the Sun Goddess Amaterasu. The shrine was originally situated near present-day Kyoto and moved here in A.D. 478. The main entrance takes you to the first *torii*, the sacred gateway that everywhere in Japan symbolizes the threshold of holy ground.

As you walk along the avenue of pines and giant cedars, you pass on the right the **Anzaisho**, the emperor's rest house, and **Sanshujo**, the rest house of his family. Beyond a second *torii* is the **Kaguraden**, Hall of the Sacred Dances. For a donation to the shrine, the *miko* (shrine maidens) in bright red pleated skirts with white blouses will perform one of the dances. The girls wield branches of the holy *sakaki* tree and dance to an orchestra of *hyoshigi* (wooden clappers), *koto* (zither), flute, *sho* (organ-pipes), the oboe-like *hichiriki* and drum.

The avenue ends at the **Shoden**, Main Shrine, enclosed by a series of four unvarnished wooden fences where Shinto priests in white robes with black belts and black lacquered clogs stand to bless worshippers as they make a silent obeisance. Only members of the imperial family are permitted beyond the second fence. The Shoden itself measures just 20 feet (6 m.) high, a little less in width, and 33 feet (10 m.) long.

The Ise shrines represent the purest form of the Shinto religion. Until the Meiji Restoration of 1868, Buddhist monks and nuns were not allowed to set foot inside the precincts. Although allowed there now, they have no role to play in the ceremonies, despite the tradition elsewhere of Shinto and Buddhism joining forces in forms of worship and architecture.

Each shrine is constructed of plain, unadorned Japanese cypress wood brought especially from the Kiso Mountains in the Central Alps north-east of Nagoya. The style of the cross-beamed roofs and simple wooden frames is the same that was used 2,000 and more years ago, before Chinese architecture exerted its influence when Buddhism arrived here from Korea.

The **Geku-Jin-en Sacred Park** at the foot of Mt. Takakura is an integral part of the sanctuary and a beautiful place for a quiet stroll. In fact, if you don't feel like taking the bus, the walk to the second shrine takes you along a delightful tree-shaded avenue lined with stone lanterns.

Naiku, the Inner Shrine, is the more important of the two, being dedicated to Amaterasu the Sun Goddess, supreme deity of the Shinto cult. The Naiku shrine, said to be founded here nearly

2,000 years ago, also holds the sacred eight-pointed mirror, *ya-ta-no-kagami*, one of the three symbols of the imperial throne (the others are the sword, kept at Atsuta Shrine in Nagoya, and the jewel, in the Imperial Palace, Tokyo). The layout of Naiku and construction of the Shoden are similar to those of the Geku, with a perhaps more picturesque approach to the Naiku over the Uji Bridge across the Isuzu River. Like the shrines, the bridge is renewed every 20 years.

The ritual dismantling, known as *sengu-shiki*, dates back to pre-historic times when sacred structures were erected only for special ceremonies, not for permanent places of worship. You'll notice beside each shrine an area of open ground on which the new shrine will be erected (next one in 1993) in identical form. The structures are broken up into small pieces and distributed to the faithful as talismans. This whole process is painstaking and expensive, and the "democratization" of the imperial institutions since the emperor renounced his divinity after World War II means that the shrines have to foot the bill instead of the state. So to defray the costs, the faith-

ful now have to make a generous donation for their talisman.

Join the Japanese visitors down at the Isuzu River where they perform a rite of purification by washing their mouths with its clear fresh waters and at the same time play with the big fat red, silver and black carp swimming around in it.

A bus from the town of Ise runs along the spectacular **Ise-**

Discover the play of light and shade in an old Takayama house.

Shima Skyline road along the ridge of Mt. Asama to the resort town of **Toba**, where a highly commercialized operation touts the cultured pearl production of Mikimoto Pearl Island. You can watch women dressed in white robes diving offshore for the artificially induced pearl oysters that make up the necklaces, trinkets and model pagodas and castles of the souvenir trade.

CHUBU

Chubu is the central region of Honshu island, stretching northeast of Kinki across the Hida, Kiso and Akaishi mountains, known collectively as the Japan Alps, to the plains of the north coast and the Sea of Japan. It's most easily explored in an excursion from the Kinki district by JR train from Nagoya. The picturesque mountain-railway

journey is a very important part of the pleasure.

In the middle of the mountains, the charming town of Takayama is well worth a visit for the rare opportunity it offers of seeing small town life in traditional style with authentic folkcrafts and handsome rustic architecture—something you won't easily see on the coastal plains where you spend most of your time. The town also serves as a good base for hikes you may like to make into the unspoiled countryside of the surrounding Japan Alps National Park.

Situated not far from the Japan Sea coast, the major town is Kanazawa, once the stronghold of the great Maeda clan and still preserving some attractive old houses of the clan's samurai warriors in the historic quarter that once nestled against the castle precincts.

Takayama

The Takayama line train, from Nagoya via Gifu, takes you along the Kiso and Hida river valleys. The leisurely three-hour ride passes through steep gorges, narrow terraced rice paddies and neatly tailored tea plantations hugging the mountain slopes with not a square inch of usable land wasted. The bright green of the rice and tea plants contrasts with the darker green of the dense primeval pine forests and groves of maple. Sturdy brown farmhouses add splashes of colour with the azaleas and peonies of their gardens. The train stops by riverside markets where farmers trade fruit and vegetables and gossip with the passengers.

Takayama is a town famous for its carpenters, going all the way back to the great days of the imperial courts of Nara and Kyoto. Too poor in the harvests of its Hida mountain district to contribute taxes to the national treasury, the town sent instead its skilful artisans—*Hida-no-takumi*—to help build the temples and palaces of the imperial capital. Those skills have been handed down to present-day craftsmen working in yew-wood, and the old timbered houses are exquisitely maintained in traditional style. The local lord in turn borrowed the capital's grid pattern when laying out medieval Takayama, which became known as "Little Kyoto".

Just as Kyoto is an appropriate place to stay in one of the grand *ryokan* inns, so Takayama would be a good town to try out familystyle *minshuku* (see p. 57)— they're especially friendly here. And you need nothing but your own two feet to get around town, though you may like to rent a bicycle at the railway station for a ride into the surrounding countryside.

Start your day with the Takayama housewives at the open-air **Asaichi** morning market down on the east bank of the Miya River north of Yasugawa Street bridge. The clear mountain air makes all the more appetizing the display of fruit and vegetables from the Hida farms and the flowers and nuts brought down from the hills.

A little back from the river, going south, you'll find the delightful **old houses** and workshops of Kami-Sannomachi and Furuimachinami streets. The craftwork here—yew-wood carvings, lacquerware and pottery—is of very high quality. Furuimachinami is quieter and more residential, with long, two-storey unpainted dark timber houses, lattice façades and low-balconied verandahs, a few flowers and shrubs in pots or *hako-niwa* box gardens to add some colour. The only "modern" note to be discerned is in the names of some of the cafés, such as Sugar Hill or Greenwich Village, offering "coffee and jazz"—very good coffee and very good jazz records in the Japan Alps.

At the southern end of Furuimachinami, cross over the river to visit the **Jinya** palace-villa that belonged to the lord of the local ruling Kanamori clan until its takeover by the Tokugawa shogunate. The handsome weathered structure has the same unadorned simplicity of the townsmen's houses. (The morning market in front of the Jinya is more of a bustle than the one down by the river.)

You should also see two **merchants' houses** just east of the riverside market, Yoshijima-ke and Kusakabe Mingeikan, the latter turned into a superb folkcraft museum. Both are imposing works of art in themselves, their massive cross-beams and pillars making dramatic patterns in their spacious interiors. The museum displays local costume, wood-carvings and the fine transparent *shunkei-nuri* lacquerware that highlights rather than conceals the grain of the wood.

The town's most important temple is the 16th-century **Kokubunji.** Next to the three-storey pagoda is a pretty gingko tree said to be over 1,000 years old.

South-east of town is **Shiroyama Park** with a pleasantly neglected look to its unlandscaped slopes covered with wild flowers and offering an extensive view of the town and the Japan Alps beyond.

Hida Minzoku-Mura is a fascinating museum-village of authentic old farmhouses from the region, most of them rescued from an area flooded by the nearby Mihoro Dam. Laid out in a pretty hillside setting half a mile south-west of Takayama Station, the steeply pitched, grass-

Peasant ladies come down from the Hida hills to sell their flowers.

thatch-roofed houses, many of three or four storeys, may remind European visitors of alpine villages back home. The houses display old farm tools and cooking utensils. Some of them operate as workshops where you can see the much-vaunted local craftsmen demonstrating their skills in lacquerwork, carving, weaving and dyeing.

Hikers and mountain-climbers will enjoy the excursion by bus (95 minutes from Takayama) to **Norikura**, a 9,928-foot (3,026-m.), cone-shaped volcano at the southern end of the Japan Alps National Park. For the hikers, as opposed to the climbers, a bus goes to a point quite close to the summit and it's an easy but exhilarating walk to the top.

Kanazawa

Largest city in northern Chubu, Kanazawa has been able to preserve its older charms from the assaults of the Tokugawa shoguns and the bombs of World War II by pursuing a peaceful career of unmenacing arts, crafts and scholarship; there is a university here, as well as an arts and crafts college.

Kenrokuen Park, a classical Edo-period "strolling" garden regarded as one of the best in Japan, makes a good place to start your visit. The park has a plethora of ponds bordered by stone lanterns, waterfalls, serpentine streams, cherry trees and pines, with artfully constructed hillocks to provide panoramic views of the landscaping. The central **Kasumigaike** ("Misty Lake") is the most attractive of the ponds, with its Tortoise Shell Island—the tortoise being much favoured by the Japanese as a symbol of long life.

South of the park is the **Noh Theatre**, for which Kanazawa is nationally famous; here you may have a better chance of seeing a performance than in Tokyo. The town has always encouraged its citizens to participate in the arts, and most of the first-rate talent is locally recruited.

Among the Kanazawans' other talents is the pretty five-colour glazed *kutani* pottery, which you'll see in many downtown shops. But take a look at the displays in the municipal **Art Museum** in the park before buying, so that you'll distinguish cheap copies.

Nagamachi is the old samurai quarter, west of the park. It's a pure delight to wander along the secluded canals among the dark timbered houses, all situated in very narrow zigzagging streets to hamper enemy attack. Notice the lovely little gardens behind the tall fences.

In the same neighbourhood, you can visit the superb **Saihitsu-an** house and watch silk-dyers at work on fabulously expensive kimono materials.

The old **geisha district,** slightly more rundown than Nagamachi but no less quaint, is on the eastern edge of town, north of the Umeno Hashi bridge across the Asano River.

Oyama Shrine, close to the university and (badly reconstructed) castle, was built in 1875 by a Dutchman whose Western touch can be seen in the neo-Renaissance arches and the stained-glass beacon for sailors on the distant Japan Sea.

A pleasant train excursion from Kanazawa (two or three hours' round trip) takes you along the rugged coast of the **Noto Peninsula**. Look out for the sleepy little fishing villages beyond the rather garish spa town of Wakura.

WESTERN HONSHU AND SHIKOKU

To discover the considerable charms of the Inland Sea, make a change from plane, train or taxi and take the ferryboat or hydrofoil, or try the longer cruises between Honshu and Shikoku island.

Along the Western Honshu coast, you can visit the castle-town of Himeji, sample the quaint and enchanting village-like atmosphere of Kurashiki and make what has become a veritable pilgrimage for Westerners to observe the spectacular rebirth of Hiroshima. From there, it's a pleasant boat ride out to the celebrated scenic beauty of Miyajima with its vermilion *torii* rising out of the sea.

Shikoku is popular with the Japanese for the annual springtime pilgrimage: mostly on foot, dressed all in white, pilgrims visit each of 88 Buddhist temples in honour of the island's great 8th-century priest Kobo-Daishi. For foreign visitors, there's the intriguing sight of the Japanese at play in the Dogo Spa at Matsuyama and the historic castle-town of Takamatsu.

Himeji

If you're heading towards Western Honshu from the Kyoto area, **Himeji Castle** makes a very worthwhile stopover for a couple of hours' visit.

All over Japan, you'll come across replicas of the grand old castles that once dominated feudal life but were then progressively destroyed by civil war, the jealousies of the Tokugawa shogunate or by the firebombs of World War II. Himeji offers the one surviving first-rate authentic example of a castle lovingly restored in its original materials, unlike slapdash reconstructions in ferroconcrete like Osaka. Himeji Castle is also a stunningly beautiful building in its own right, combining military effectiveness with architectural elegance. It's justifiably known as the "White Heron Castle" for the way its swooping, white, gabled silhouette gracefully soars over the modern skyline of Himeji. It's an easy walk along the town's main thoroughfare leading directly from the station.

There's been a fortress in Himeji dominating the Harima Plain since the 14th century, but the castle in its present form dates from the early 1600s. Its heyday came when the triumvirate of Nobunaga, Hideyoshi and Tokugawa put an end to the 16th-century civil wars. Hideyoshi used Himeji as a base of operations against the recalcitrant warlords of Western Honshu.

The castle is admired by military historians as being the most complex and ingenious of Japanese castle designs. It's a "hillock castle", *hirayama jiro* (as opposed to flatlands, mountainside or waterside castles), with the mound on which its tower-keep is built coming from the earth dug out of three ranks of spiralling moats. The elaborate fortifications are completed by a series of external, intermediate and interior ramparts.

Without the benefit of the signposts directing the modern visitor, the enemy could reach the Daitenshu main castle-keep only through an impossible labyrinth of twisting pathways, dryland gates and water gates. Thus it's not surprising when you come across one last enclosure next to the inner courtyard, popularly known as Harakiri-no-maru ("Suicide Yard").

The castle includes attractive displays of weapons, armour and costumes of the feudal era. Notice, too, the different clan seals of the castle's succeeding lords, at the ends of the fluted roofs of the gables—the butterfly of Himeji's principal builder, Terumasa Ikeda, the inevitable hollyhock of the Tokugawa and the cross of a Christian convert, Yoshitaka Kuroda.

You can see the **Kesho Yagura** ("Vanity Tower") reserved for Ieyasu Tokugawa's notorious *femme fatale* granddaughter Senhime after she married the lord of the castle and paid for most of its construction with her dowry. Best of all is the view from the top of the five-storey **Daitenshu** castle-keep, especially the close-up look you get of the 11 great *shachihoko* ornamental dolphin tails on the gable roofs, performing the same ritual anti-fire function as the *shibi* bird-tails on Buddhist temples.

Kurashiki

Surrounded by heavily industrialized suburbs, the prettiness of the old centre of Kurashiki around its canals lined with dreamy willow trees provides its own reverse comment on the horrors of war. It is practically the *only* town of any consequence along this Inland Sea coast to have emerged unscathed from the terrible fire-bombings of 1945 and shows just how gracious provincial life was in prewar Japan.

In the era of the Tokugawa shoguns, the canals were used to carry rice and grain in barges for onward shipment to the great markets of Osaka and Edo. The elegant black-brick granaries have been beautifully preserved to house the town's many museums of art, folkcraft and archaeology. You'll certainly find a day's visit a very welcome change from the relentless modernity of some of the other nearby cities.

Take a short taxi ride from the

station to the museum district and do the rest on foot. There are half a dozen museums tucked into an elbow of the canal, but not all of them are of equal quality, so be sure to note down their Japanese names for when you ask your way around.

One of the most delightful is the **Kurashiki Mingeikan** folk art museum, displaying not only Japanese, Korean and Chinese pottery, glassware, textiles and bambooware, but also American Indian and European peasant ceramics and basketry with which to compare the Asian art. Other highlights in this complex of four remodelled granaries are farmhouse furniture and utensils and the costumes of the Ainu people whose few survivors live up north in Hokkaido.

On the other hand, the **Ohara Bijutsukan** art museum is a collection, in what looks like a Greek temple, of rather poor examples of Western art by such illustrious names as Cézanne, Degas, Van Gogh and El Greco. It does, however, have the curiosity value of one Japanese collector's view of Western art, and Mr. Ohara is to be thanked for having financed the conservation of the granaries as museums. His **Ohara Tokikan Pottery Hall** is a much more satisfying collection, devoted to the work of modern pottery masters Kanjiro Kawai, Shoji Hamada and Kenkichi Tomimo-to, as well as their much admired British friend, Bernard Leach.

The **Kurashiki Bijutsukan** municipal art museum houses the Ninagawa family's admirable collection of ancient Greek, Egyptian, Roman and Persian ceramics, sculpture and mosaics, 19th-century French and Italian marble and bronze sculptures and some astonishing Rococo porcelain from Meissen, Vienna, Berlin and Sèvres. Just to remind you you're in Japan, you'll find a completely furnished traditional Japanese living room on the fourth floor.

If you've become a great fan of the large "strolling" gardens, the 18th-century **Korakuen** in the nearby town of Okayama is considered a must by connoisseurs. It's particularly pleasant to sample the tea ceremony amid the cherry and plum trees on one side of the pavilion in the spring or the gorgeous maples on the other side in the autumn. Across the Asahi River, there's a nice view of the ruins of Okayama Castle, painted black and called "The Crow" (*ujo*) in deliberate contrast to Himeji's "White Heron Castle".

"Thousand-crane" ribbons protect Hiroshima babies yet to be born.

Hiroshima

One of your first thoughts as the train rolls past the sign HIRO-SHIMA on the station platform may well be: "It really is there". Around the station, you see skyscrapers, neon signs, cars zipping along the highway—a living town. It's of course well known by now that one of the citizens' many inspired acts of psychotherapy was to start reconstruction as soon as the dust had settled, but that knowledge may not overcome the simple reflex of wonder. This was a town that had been wiped, as they say, from the face of the earth. The very name "Hiroshima" quite simply evokes total obliteration, so it's an inevitable shock to see anything there at all.

What is there, in fact, is a bright and bustling city of broad avenues and green and plea-

sant parkland, prosperous, well-dressed citizens—approaching a million, much more than double the figure in World War II.

When you walk around the crowded city centre, you may find yourself looking at this or that old man or woman to guess what age they were on August 6, 1945, imagining what they were doing at the moment of the "Flash"—as they call the atomic explosion—at 8.15 a.m.

The people of Hiroshima do not shy away from the particular burden history has shouldered them with, but with characteristic Japanese discretion and reserve, their **Peace Memorial Park** is movingly simple, eloquent without overt passion. (The park is a 1-mile tram ride south-west of Hiroshima Station. Take the No. 1 tram to Chuden-mae stop and walk to the park across Peace Bridge.)

The **Peace Memorial Museum** documents the horror with charts, photographs, video films, sound recordings in most European languages and, especially effectively, with the charred remains of clothing, everyday utensils and twisted masonry. The most evocative document is one isolated photograph, a human shadow left imprinted on the steps of the Sumitomo Bank at the moment of the "Flash". The country's best architects such as Kenzo Tange designed the var-

ious monuments—the **Cenotaph** with its 108,956 names and inscription: "Let all the souls here rest in peace, for the evil shall not be repeated"; the starkly simple museum; and the huge bronze **Peace Bell**. But the most eloquent testimony comes at the north end of the park from the one building left standing since 1945, the Hiroshima Prefectural Industrial Promotion Hall, now known as the **Atomic Bomb Dome**. This clumsy, undistinguished chamber of commerce building stands today still gutted by the blast (and ironically propped up against further collapse by new steel girders), its new name derived from the skeletal iron cupola. It's still surrounded by its old rubble, but also by the cherry trees and pink azaleas of any self-respecting Japanese park. The dubious privilege of having stood at the epicentre of the world's first atomic bomb has not deprived it of a certain nobility as a simple work of man.

Since the people of Hiroshima are not reluctant to discuss the past, you may find it salutary rather than morbid to choose this city in which to participate in the "Home Visit Programme" (see p. 56), organized here by the Hiroshima City Tourist Association, with offices on the north-east side of the park.

The city planners have done everything possible to make the

park itself a dignified setting for this memorial to catastrophe. In the context, it would not be undignified for you to seek a therapeutic antidote in the lively shopping centres east of the park around Hondori, Hachobori and Kamiya-cho.

Miyajima

Also known as Itsukushima, after its waterside shrine, Miyajima island is one of the country's most popular tourist spots, so it's an especially good idea to make a very early start to beat the crowds. (Some 25 minutes from Hiroshima to Miyajima-guchi Station by JR train and 10 minutes by ferry-boat to the island.)

Not even the most blasé sightseer can deny the striking beauty of the **Itsukushima Shrine**'s bright red camphorwood *torii* rising 52 feet (16 m.) out of the sea in front of the long low black and red buildings of the shrine, itself built on stilts to jut out over the water.

Founded perhaps as far back as the 6th century, the shrine's sanctity is such that, until the modernization that came with the Meiji era after 1868, pregnant mothers and serious invalids were carried to the mainland so that there should be no births or deaths on the island. Mourners had to undergo 50 days of purification before being

allowed back on Miyajima. While most of these religious laws have been relaxed, burials are still not permitted here.

But, characteristic of Japanese religious practice, the atmosphere on Miyajima manages nonetheless to be both solemn and cheerful. Sacred *bugaku* and *kagura* dances are performed, in exchange for spectators' donations to the shrine, and the souvenir shops do a great business in local woodcarvings, sacred and profane. You'll find handsome polished cedarwood cups, bowls and trays, but also monstrously ugly versions of the deer and monkeys to be seen darting around the hills behind the shrine.

You can escape the crowds by hiking up the wild but clear and easily negotiable trail to the sum-

---

A Rye Scoop
One peculiar souvenir item on Miyajima is the wooden rice-scoop on which the Japanese write the address and stick a stamp to send through the mail as a talisman for their dear ones. Many of them may not realize now that it was soldiers garrisoned on Miyajima who started the craze prior to their military expedition against the Chinese in 1894. The rice-scoops denoted a play on words in which meshi-toru meant "scoop up rice" or "conquer China".

mit of 1,739-foot (530-m.) **Mt. Misen** (most people pay to take the ropeway). The forest is a sheer delight and, past the secluded Gumonjido Buddhist temple, the **view** from the top over the Inland Sea to Hiroshima is a grand bonus.

Shikoku

Although it's the biggest town on Shikoku island, **Matsuyama** (hydrofoil from Hiroshima via Kure) is a pleasantly quiet place, serving principally as the shopping centre for the jolly folk visiting the hot springs just 2½ miles (4 km.) away. **Dogo Spa** is a great place to try out the public bathhouse. Don your *yukata* cotton kimono and go native—clogs, too, if you can manage them. The spring water is alkaline and crystal clear and good for stomach ailments, the lungs and the nervous system. What more could you ask?

Nicely unlandscaped, **Shiroyama Park** covers the lovely wooded slopes of Katsuyama Hill, dominated by the neatly preserved **Matsuyama Castle** that was once the redoubt of the Matsudaira *daimyo*. This most faithful lieutenant of the Tokugawa clan distinguished himself by planting

Itsukushima's 600-year-old pagoda fends off the salty sea air with a fresh lick of paint every year.

the cedar forest around the shoguns' mausoleums at Nikko (see p. 75). He was doubtless inspired by the forests of his Matsuyama home.

Just a mile from Dogo Spa is the 14th-century **Ishiteji Temple**, one of the 88 stages of the springtime Buddhist pilgrimage around Shikoku. Notice particularly the handsome Niomon Gate.

Takamatsu (at the eastern end of Shikoku, directly across the Inland Sea from Kurashiki and Okayama) is also a friendly provincial town where foreigners seem to receive an especially warm welcome. The citizens are very proud of their **Ritsurin Park**, with its bizarre twisted pines and grotesquely shaped boulders. The folk art museum here is worth a visit, but above all, the park offers a gracious and unpretentious tea ceremony at the delightful **Kiku-getsu-tei** pavilion. The view out on to the pavilion's little rock and white gravel gardens is a classic of the genre.

A 20-minute tram ride takes you out to **Yashima** peninsula, formerly an island, famous for the momentous battles in which the Minamoto clan drove out their Taira rivals in 1182, heralding the country's rule by military dictatorship for the next seven centuries. Ruins of the Taira clan's dwellings are still visible, and Yashimaji Temple houses relics of the battles.

KYUSHU

The south-westernmost of Japan's four main islands, Kyushu has always set itself apart from the others, both in its climate, which is distinctly Mediterranean and even subtropical at its southern tip, and in its often fiercely independent-minded and more emotional people—perhaps conditioned by their warmer weather.

Easily accessible from the Asian mainland via Korea, Kyushu has been more susceptible to foreign influences than the rest of Japan, particularly after it found itself on the southern route taken by the European merchants and missionaries of the 16th century. Even today, the people of Kyushu remain noticeably more open and friendly to foreigners, going beyond the formal courtesies which you are most likely to encounter on Honshu island.

Kyushu is proud that, both in the national mythology and in the meagre archaeologically certifiable facts, it was here that the colonization of Japan had its earliest beginnings. Legend says it was on Mt. Takachiho in central Kyushu that Sun Goddess Amaterasu sent her grandson with the imperial mirror, sword and jewel with which Japan's first Emperor Jimmu was to set out on his conquest of the Yamato Plain around Nara. One of the modern historians' best guesses is that the historical Jimmu was probably a pirate from Okinawa who settled in Kyushu before launching his assault on Honshu.

The island's next important encounter with history was as the target of the abortive invasions by the Mongols under Kublai Khan in 1274 and 1281. The islanders' heroic resistance, admittedly abetted by a timely typhoon fatally dubbed *kamikaze* ("Divine Wind"), established Kyushu's enduring military tradition. The island proved to be the last bastion of the samurai ideal. It was in Kagoshima that the Imperial Japanese Navy was created from the nucleus of ships bought from the British by the local Shimazu clan at the end of the 19th century.

Portuguese merchants arrived in Kagoshima in 1543 and the missionaries of St. Francis Xavier quickly followed. Nagasaki became a centre of Western trade and a Japanese foothold for the Catholic Church, which has revived today after the 250 years of suppression under the Tokugawa shoguns.

The highly volatile island abounds in hot spring resorts, such as Unzen in the Unzen-Amakusa National Park, Beppu with its famous "boiling hell" mud pots, or Ibusuki, where you can bury yourself in hot volcanic sands. If you like something more active, there's golf and other sports at Miyazaki and, most active of all, Mt. Aso, one of the world's largest regularly erupting volcanoes, rises in the centre of Kyushu. In the south, Mt. Sakurajima, too, sends out spectacular mushroom clouds, raining a little daily dose of black ash over Kagoshima. Like Kagoshima, Kumamoto is a delightfully green city with a fascinating bellicose history. And you should not miss the port-city of Nagasaki, a still lovely cosmopolitan town that emerged from its atomic holocaust in much better shape than Hiroshima.

Travel to Kyushu is most convenient by air, one hour 40 minutes from Tokyo to the island's main gateway, Fukuoka, or seven hours by *shinkansen* to Fukuoka's Hakata Station. If you can afford the "bullet train" only once, this would be the most advantageous time to do it, taking you on one exhilarating sweep through almost all the major cities of Central and Western Honshu on the way.

Northern Kyushu

Fukuoka itself is Kyushu's biggest commercial centre. You can visit the lively and prosperous shopping district around the main station at **Hakata**—the *Hakata-ningyo* dolls, speciality craft of the town, make attractive gifts, for adults rather than children.

155

But otherwise, you'll just be passing through on your way south.

First stop on the east coast is bouncing **Beppu**, perhaps the busiest, certainly the most vigorously self-promotional spa town in Japan, with a permanent population of just 150,000, but claiming 13 million visitors a year. The Beppu district boasts eight different hot springs, each with different natural chemical properties. To justify the slogan "You've got it, we'll cure it", they have a hot waterfall at the Shibaseki spring, hot sand at Takegawara, hot mud at Kannawa and picturesque outdoor baths in hot ponds among the rocks of nicely named Hotta Hot Springs.

The tour of the **"hell ponds"** around Kannawa is hilarious. In the open-air Umi Jigoku, "Ocean Hell", they'll boil eggs for you in a basket. It's worth the 3½-minute wait. Bozu Jigoku, "Monk's Hell", is just one big obscenely bubbling mud pond where a Buddhist temple once stood until submerged in an earthquake back in the 15th century. In Oniyama Jigoku, "Devil's Mountain Hell", a hundred crocodiles enjoy a hot soak. Chinoike Jigoku is "Blood Pool Hell", a steaming pond turned blood red by its iron oxide.

To get into the swing of things, join the Japanese at the grand old Meiji-era Takegawara public baths around 7.30 p.m.

The countryside around Beppu is delightful—splendid hikes on the **Kijima Plateau**, strawberry picking in springtime, all-year-round hang-gliding from **Mt. Tsurumi** down to Lake Shidaka. And to get well away from the madding crowd, head southwest over Mt. Tsurumi to the enchanting little country village of **Yufuin**. After the modern city of Beppu, this is a trip back to another century, among old-fashioned farmhouses around the little Kinrinko ("Golden Fish-Scale") Lake. In this rustic setting at the foot of Mt. Yufu, an extinct volcano covered by dense bamboo forest, a visit to the 12th-century thatch-roofed Bussanji Buddhist temple or its contemporary Shinto shrine Unagihime, surrounded by a small moat, is no longer a cultural duty, just sheer contemplative pleasure. The folkcraft museum in an old manor house is worth a look, too.

A short excursion north of Beppu takes you to **Usa** to the nationally revered 8th-century hillside Shinto shrine, beautifully ensconced in a subtropical forest of bamboo. But ask, too, for the nearby Tokoji Temple's **Gohyaku Rakan**, "Grove of 500 Disciples of Buddha", a remarkable series of stone sculptures, each with a strikingly individual expression: smiling, sad, pensive, ironic, disillusioned, even downright malicious. It is said we can all find our own faces if we look hard enough there among the camphor trees. Beyond the grove, you'll also find 16 more elaborately sculpted Buddhas, one having just slain a dragon in a very St. George-like pose.

On the way back to Beppu, if you're still in the mood for a hike up through a cool forest, take a look at the Buddha heads and two fierce Heavenly Guardians carved out of the **Kumano Cliff**, very rare examples of such rock sculpture in Japan, here in a lovely setting beside a mountain stream.

The thick groves of palm trees that line the coast at **Miyazaki**

Had enough of the hot springs? Try shell-hunting on the beach.

make it quite clear that the tropics are not far. This resort town has a long and usually uncrowded sandy beach and there are several very pretty golf courses among the palm trees. **Heiwadai Park** brings together the prehistoric past and the still uncomfortable present. The park's Prefectural Museum displays small *haniwa* clay figures found at nearby ancient burial mounds, along with pots, tools and weapons dating back to 10,000 B.C. But the grounds are dominated by the bizarre and grandiose Peace Tower, which, you may be surprised to learn, was erected in 1940. But at the time, it had a different name, Hakko-ichi-wu, "Eight World Regions Under One Roof", representing the war aims of the Japanese Army. More honourable in its intentions is the park's **Miyazaki Shrine**, dedicated to the country's historico-legendary first emperor, Jimmu, who started his triumphant career in these parts.

South of the town, the little island of **Aoshima** is popular with young lovers, and its palm trees do indeed make a romantic South Seas backdrop for a picnic. Be-

Bizarre natural rock-formations along the coast of Miyazaki.

yond Aoshima, the picturesque winding Nichinan coast alternates rugged cliffs with some fine sandy bathing beaches. **Udo Shrine**, some 30 miles (50 km.) south of Miyazaki, is unique among Shinto sanctuaries for its setting in a grotto down at the water's edge surrounded by grotesque wind-stunted cactus, waving palms and strange bulbous rock formations washed by crashing breakers. The shrine carvings include some equally strange elephants, dragons and lions.

The seafood along this coast is especially good—try the reasonably priced lobster and giant winkles.

Southern Kyushu

Kagoshima dominates the head of a deep indentation at the southern tip of Kyushu, and its harbour has played a pre-eminent role in Japanese military history. It was here that the Portuguese landed, bringing to Japan for the first time bread, guns and Christianity. The sailors' first landfall was on the little offshore island of Tanegashima, which has progressed from muskets and matchlocks to Japan's principal rocket-launching centre.

The town was the home of the powerful Shimazu clan which ruled this Satsuma region for seven centuries, remaining almost completely autonomous

even during the Tokugawa shogunate. They put up fierce resistance to foreign incursions in the 19th century, but they showed pragmatic foresight after an attack by the British Navy flattened Kagoshima: the lord of the Shimazu immediately negotiated with the enemy to purchase some of those fiendishly effective battleships to create in Kagoshima the basis of the future Japanese Imperial Navy.

The town also served as the base from which was launched the Satsuma Rebellion, famous last stand of the samurai against the overthrow of their time-honoured privileges. And it was from here that began the last desperate sorties of World War II to resist the American invasion, including the *kamikaze* raids on U.S. warships. Inevitably, devastating bombing reprisals again flattened the city, but modern Kagoshima is now an attractive green and airy place with wide boulevards, lovely parks and a couple of intriguing historical museums.

Shiroyama Park (south-west of Kagoshima Station) is up on a hill, giving you a fine view of the city and Kagoshima Bay through the *torii* of **Nanshu Shrine**. This shrine is dedicated to Kyushu's most celebrated son and one of Japan's national heroes, Takamori Saigo, last great champion of the samurai. He is buried with

2,023 of his warriors, many of them suicides like himself, who died in the 1877 Satsuma Rebellion.

A **museum** in the park is devoted to his life and battles. It is worth spending some time here to ponder the fascinating phenomenon of the samurai, a feudal institution that formally died out little more than a century ago, but seems to live on in spirit among the warriors' descendants, either very explicitly with sumo wrestlers and practitioners of the martial arts, or implicitly in the solemn dedication of Japan's new heroes, the businessmen.

The modernity Saigo resisted is celebrated at the bottom of Shiroyama Hill in another shrine, **Terukuni**, dedicated to Nariakira Shimazu, lord of Satsuma. It was he who launched the enduring national craze for photography, as well as bringing to Kyushu the benefits of telegraphy and new techniques of cotton-spinning.

The whole history of the Kagoshima region is nicely resumed in the ultra-modern **Reimeikan** Prefectural Museum near by, including local arts and crafts and some of those first Portuguese matchlock rifles.

A couple of miles north of Kagoshima Station are the lovely **Iso Gardens**, also landscaped on a hill, where the lord of Satsuma had his villa. Be sure to visit the **Shoko Shuseikan Museum**, housed in an old factory established here by the forward-looking leader for arms manufacture and other new industries. Among

---

Napoleon, Washington and Dogs
Takamori Saigo's popularity seems to derive from his combination of spartanly simple tastes, a superb common touch with his men and noble dedication to traditional values. "Respect heaven, love the people" was his motto. He distrusted the duplicity of the general run of humanity and preferred dogs—practically every statue of him in the parks around the country shows him with his pet pug.

Although he was a fervent patriot who died fighting the influx of foreign ideas, his heroes were Napoleon and George Washington. After participating in the overthrow of the Tokugawa shogunate to restore the symbolic authority of his beloved emperor, he was disillusioned by the new politicians who were overturning his honourable traditions in their haste to dismantle the machinery of feudalism. When his Satsuma Rebellion failed to halt the process of modernization—using the now forbidden swords against the new guns of the Imperial Army—Saigo committed suicide. The museum shows his black uniform adorned only with the Satsuma emblem and the crisscross slashes left by his harakiri.

the historical artefacts on display are two fascinating documents: the very first Japanese photograph (just think what an avalanche that started), a portrait of Nariakira Shimazu himself, taken in 1857, one year before his death; and another photograph, of the first eight Kagoshima exchange students who went to London in 1865, immaculately dressed in suits good enough for the common room of any decent British public school.

Not all Shimazu lords were as bright as Nariakira. You can still see where one of his predecessors had three gigantic Chinese characters chiselled out of a rock on the tree-covered cliff above the gardens, spelling *sen-jin-gan*, meaning "a huge rock".

Out in the bay, towering over a whole peninsula, is the big three-coned **Sakurajima** volcano, very active indeed, sending up tremendous black and white clouds of ash and steam. Take a taxi or bus (from Kagoshima Station) for a close-up look at the lava and incidentally a fine **view** of the whole Kagoshima Bay area. The Sakurajima peninsula was once an island until the gigantic eruption of 1914, when the rocks and lava it spewed forth joined it to the mainland. For a more graphic idea of the magnitude of the eruption, look out for Haragosha Shrine, where you can just see the top cross bar of the shrine's *torii*, the rest of it submerged by lava.

Quite volcanic in effect is the local *imo-jochu* brew, distilled from yams and more potent in impact than *sake*. Visit the **Honbo-shuzo distillery** to see it made —and sample some in the factory's own restaurant (a half-hour bus ride from Kagoshima Station).

St. Francis Xavier's Memorial Church in Xavier Park (tram to Takamibaba stop) was built in 1949 on the 400th anniversary of his arrival here. His statue, strangely pinned halfway up a monolith in very martyr-like pose, though he died in his bed (in China), stands with its back to the sea beside a sculpted frieze dedicated to the suffering of his Japanese converts.

At **Ibusuki**, due south of Kagoshima, Japanese togetherness when on holiday takes on a special dimension. This hot spring resort has made big business out of catering to honeymoon couples, hundreds of them at a time —though ordinary mortals are also allowed. For some reason, the newlyweds are not interested in separating themselves from the rest of mankind during those first precious days of matrimony. The public baths of the main

Sakurajima guarantees an eruption almost every day of the year.

hotel are a major theatrical attraction, with an elaborate decor of indoor palm trees and waterfalls. In the sports-arena-sized dining hall, floor shows of Hawaiian hula dancers and fire-eaters add another touch of exotica.

But the best show of all is outside on Ibusuki's **Surigahama Beach** where, clad only in your *yukata* cotton kimono, you lie down for attendants to bury you up to the neck in sand that's toasting hot from the underground volcanic activity. Just stare up at the moon and the stars and sweat off a few pounds of fat or ease the travel aches while the attendant heats up the treatment by shovelling on fresh sand. As the local chamber of commerce puts it: "It is not only effective for overall beauty, but also for whiplash injuries caused by traffic accidents, and popular with newlyweds."

Chiran (80 minutes inland by bus from Kagoshima) is a peaceful secluded 18th-century samurai village. In classically narrow, zigzagging lanes to hinder surprise attack, the houses, still inhabited by the Satsuma warriors' descendants, offer the rare opportunity of visiting some exquisite private gardens, otherwise carefully concealed behind tall hedges. The simple serene style of landscaping, with rocks, gravel and a few shrubs, draws on the precepts of the Zen Buddhism which had a special appeal for the austere samurai.

Six gardens in all are open to visitors (who remain noticeably quieter and more respectful here than in the temples of Kyoto). Look out especially for the **Rioyichi Hirayama** house (second on the right as you walk up from the village hospital), with its superb use of the *shakkei* technique of "borrowed landscape", incorporating in its layout of rocky pond, pink azaleas and dark green hedge the distant slopes of Mt. Hahagatake, covered with a forest of pine and bamboo.

It was the tradition-laden tranquillity of Chiran that prompted its choice as the last residential quarters of the *kamikaze* "special attack corps" before they set off on their suicidal missions to strike one last blow at the advancing American forces in 1945. A **Kamikaze Museum** with a monumental statue of a pilot exhibits the young men's uniforms, helmets and their last letters to their families explaining how they were continuing the samurai spirit of defending the country's traditional values. There are also full-scale models of the planes, with a fuel tank big enough only for a one-way mission.

Be sure the hot-sand bath attendant doesn't forget your toes.

165

Western Kyushu

Halfway back up Kyushu's west coast, **Kumamoto** is an old castle town, of considerable importance to the Tokugawa shoguns as a counterweight to the too independent-minded Shimazu clan down in Kagoshima. For visitors today, Kumamoto serves as a convenient gateway for the pretty road trip to the Mt. Aso volcano or ferry cruise to the Unzen-Amakusa National Park.

But the reconstructed **Kumamoto Castle** is worth a visit for its significance in the last hectic days of Japan's feudal era. Once a vast fortification of 49 turrets, it ranked with Osaka and Nagoya as one of the country's greatest impregnable bastions. The 1960 ferroconcrete reconstruction of the main castle-keep houses a fine museum of feudal armour and weapons and offers a good view of the city. The castle's glory came to an end in 1877 during the Satsuma Rebellion, when it was besieged by Takamori Saigo and his men. Before they were forced to withdraw against the Imperial Army's superior strength, their assaults had destroyed practically everything but the massive stone ramparts and a few exterior turrets.

One of the few surviving structures of Kumamoto Castle is the Tsukimi Yagura, "Moon-Viewing Tower", facing south. It was occupied during the siege by the Satsuma samurai. In the face of almost certain defeat, but secure in the belief of the justice of their cause, the warriors passed the time singing patriotic songs, writing melancholy poems and looking at the moon.

Suizenji Park is an extravagant but attractive example of the extensive gardens of the 17th century, reproducing in this case a miniature version of all the major landscape features along the old Tokaido Highway between Kyoto and Edo, including a small artificial version of Mt. Fuji.

Kumamoto is much appreciated by Japanese gourmets, but a lot of the *sukiyaki* you get here is horsemeat, considered a great delicacy. Have it with a little carafe of the powerful local *imo jochu* yam liquor and you'll quickly overcome your sensibilities about eating man's loyal friend.

The bus ride from Kumamoto to the great **Mt. Aso** volcano takes you across some gently rolling hills, orange groves, fields of watermelon and the special grass used for *tatami* mats, and a rare sight of yellow wheat-

The population is dense, even in a remote Unzen fishing-village.

fields—for beer and noodles, rather than bread (which is mostly imported ready-made). The panorama of the five volcanic craters of Mt. Aso blends vivid emerald green mounds with great carpets of pink azaleas on the surrounding slopes and plateau. Only one of the craters, **Nakadake**, is still really active but that is well worth a visit to the top (short hike from the bus stop) to peer down into its bleak barren crater emitting a puff of sulphurous fumes and contrasting starkly with the colourful vegetation all around it.

On your way back down, visit the first-class **Aso Volcanic Museum**. It has some very realistic audio-visual re-enactments of huge eruptions and earthquakes in quadrophonic sound. Three-dimensional models of crumbling mountains and molten lava flow from all over the world are shown. Press a button and see America's Mt. St. Helens blow its top or relive the astonishing 1933 eruption of Aso itself. One room is a laboratory of Kumamoto University in which you can see video screens monitoring live action direct from Nakadake, where cameras have been placed inside the crater. They play some music at the end of the tour to reassure frightened children—and adults.

The **Unzen-Amakusa National Park**, a peninsula and islands west of Kumamoto, is most pleasantly reached on a very pretty one-hour ferry trip from the nearby port of Misumi to Shimabara. The harbour is dotted with the lovely little pine-covered islands of Tsukumo—delightful bathing along the white sand beaches.

The serene-looking white castle of **Shimabara**, now a museum, was the scene of a bloody massacre in 1637, when 38,000 Japanese Christians—men, women and children—took refuge there from the persecutions of the Tokugawa regime. Their spiritual leader was a 16-year-old boy, Shiro Masuda, but the two and a half month military resistance, forcing the shogun to send 120,000 men to overcome it, was led by a converted samurai, Shigemasa Itakura. It is said that all the rebels perished in the slaughter.

The battlefields and tombs of the martyrs are to be found all round Shimabara and on many of the 70 **Amakusa Islands**. Old Catholic chapels and churches show where Christianity continued a quiet clandestine existence for over two centuries before daring to resurface with the Meiji Restoration. Combine a tour of these historical curiosities with some honest-to-goodness *dolce far niente* on the beautiful uncrowded beaches. You can hire a boat out to the more remote little islands, but the bigger ones are linked by a series of five bridges, making an agreeable bus ride all the way back, if you wish, to Misumi.

Unzen, once the favoured "hill station" of Europeans escaping the steaming summers of the Asian mainland, is now a rather noisy crowded spa resort. It's best used for an overnight stay prior to an early morning hike around Unzen volcano's craters. They are lovely. The volcano last erupted in spring 1991, but is not thought to be a great risk.

How about a nice egg boiled in the Unzen hot springs?

Nagasaki

Nagasaki is for many people the most charming city in all Japan. In great part, this is because it has an unbroken experience of more than four centuries of hospitality to foreigners—Chinese, Portuguese and Dutch, and now all-comers—over a period in Japanese history when outright hostility or at least profound suspicion was the rule, with an occasional arm's-length respect as the exception. But it is also physically a very attractive town. Its natural harbour surrounded by green hills is one of the most beautiful in the world, and most of its older neighbourhoods, thanks to their particular geographical situation in a protective basin, managed to survive the terrible destruction wrought by that second atomic bomb to be dropped on Japan, on August 9, 1945. This despite the fact that the Nagasaki bomb was more powerful than the one dropped on Hiroshima three days earlier.

Long before the arrival of the first Europeans, Nagasaki had been a major focus of Japan's trade with China. The Chinese influence in the city is most noticeable to this day. Major Buddhist temples, profiting from the clampdown on Christianity in the 17th century, were established by Chinese Zen monks and are designed in the style of the late Ming dynasty. On an every-

day level, the most popular Nagasaki lunch is a solid, nourishing bowl of *chanpon*, Chinese noodles in a tangy fish broth.

The Portuguese presence in the city is marked by the monument to 26 Christian martyrs executed in 1597 at the beginning of Japan's repression of Catholicism. St. Francis Xavier and the Jesuit missionaries who followed him had hitherto been received in Nagasaki with remarkable tolerance. Even after the persecution, the banishment of missionaries and the prohibition of the practice of Christianity, Nagasaki Catholics were able to continue clandestine observance throughout the years of the Tokugawa shogunate. They even went to Buddhist temples to worship the feminine Kannon deities, which were now sculpted holding a child, assimilated to Mary and Jesus.

The Dutch, being non-proselytizing Protestant businessmen, were permitted to stay on throughout the centuries of isolationism, their little community on the island of Dejima in Nagasaki Bay being the only group of foreigners left in the country. Nagasaki's *Oranda-san* (Hollanders) became the accepted word for *all* foreigners, and the

The Nagasaki Christian martyrs illuminated by stained glass.

Dutch red-brick and clapboard houses on Hollander Slope are an enduring monument to their privileged position.

One foreigner who never did come to Nagasaki, despite the efforts of tourist promoters to make us believe he did, was American Lieutenant Pinkerton, hero of Puccini's opera *Madam Butterfly*. A British merchant's home, Glover House, may have served as the model for Puccini's setting, but that's about it.

To get a good sense of Nagasaki's personality, start down at the **harbour**. Near the main railway station is a busy fish market, as always at its best early in the morning when it does brisk business in the local silver sardines and mackerel, but also in more exotic fare all laid out with artistic care.

Boat tours begin from the pier at Ohata Port Terminal, taking you on a fascinating 50-minute cruise around Nagasaki Bay. Your fair-sized excursion steamer will feel like a walnut shell as it passes the gigantic supertankers of the Mitsubishi Shipyard. Now the biggest private shipyard in the world, this is what the United States Air Force was aiming at and missed when they dropped their second atomic bomb.

Back on dry land, immediately south of the Ohata Terminal, is **Dejima Pier**, now reclaimed as part of the mainland from what

was once the Dutch island-concession (itself originally man-made, too). None of the 17th-century houses remain, but the **museum** has some interesting relics of the Dutch community. In front of the museum is a model of the neat and tidy, very Dutch little settlement they established back in 1609 when the only Japanese permitted to visit them were their trading partners and prostitutes.

To see how the Dutch of a later era lived, climb the cobbled street of **Hollander Slope** (number 5 tram to Ishibashi stop), where you'll see some red-brick and wooden clapboard houses with colonial-style verandahs and, rare sight hereabouts, chimneys. The houses may remind Americans of New England country houses, many of which were built by Dutch settlers, too. The top of the slope affords a good view of the city and tree-covered hills across the bay.

The British presence in 19th-century Nagasaki is nobly displayed at the hillside **Glover Gardens**, half a mile west of Hollander Slope. Escalators take you up to the houses of British traders. To the delighted curiosity of Japanese visitors, the houses are filled with Victorian paraphernalia—for instance damask-covered furniture, an upright piano, massive mahogany sideboard, and a grand old gramophone with big horn, manufactured by the Nippon-Ophone Company. An old Dock House, once an elegant lodging house for sailors, has been moved up the hill from the Mitsubishi Shipyard to house a nice little naval museum with fine models of old Chinese junks beside the latest Japanese oil tankers. The gardens' centrepiece is **Glover House**, home of Scottish merchant Thomas Blake Glover. Tomisaburo Kuraba, as he became for the Japanese, made his fortune selling guns to the new Meiji government.

Even if they can't convince us that Pinkerton and Madam Butterfly actually strolled through Glover Gardens, the garden designers offer an inimitably Japanese approach to Italian opera. Beside a statue of Japanese *prima donna* Tamaki Miura, who won fame as the lady left in the lurch, a series of fountains spout water from holes which trace the musical score of a Puccini aria.

Kofukuji Temple (number 5 tram to Kokaido-mae stop) is the first of the Zen Buddhist temples built by the Chinese (1620) after the Tokugawa shoguns had outlawed Christianity and ordered citizens to register as Buddhists. In a picturesque setting with palm trees in the courtyard, the temple's architecture and sculpture are typical of southern China. The Divine Guardians of the Buddha in Maso Hall, for example, one peering out and the other listening with a smile for danger, are noticeably more benign-looking than their usual ferocious Japanese counterparts. And the statues of the temple's abbots have mandarin moustaches. One of the great attractions of Kofukuji (by advance reservation) is the frugal but tasty vegetarian meal cooked by the priests themselves. Meal times are announced by the beating of a big red wooden fish-gong.

Pride and joy of the neighbourhood is the **Meganebashi**, a double-arched, stone "spectacles" bridge across the Nakajima River, built in 1634 by the abbot of Kofukuji and oldest of its kind in the country. The narrow streets bordering the river are full of little workshops where the local coral and tortoiseshell products are made and sold.

Sofukuji Temple (1629) is a handsome example of late Ming-dynasty architecture, with a striking vermilion-painted, stone-arched tower gate. In the courtyard you'll see a huge iron cauldron that was used for distributing rice-gruel to the poor during famines in the 17th and 19th centuries. The Chinese Buddha statues here are notable for their variously proud, cheerful or humble stances not to be seen in the Buddhas of Japanese temples.

173

The **Monument of the 26 Christian Martyrs** (5 minutes' walk from Nagasaki Station, at Nishizakamachi) has become a place of pilgrimage for many of the 900,000 Japanese Christians freely exercising their faith today. Hideyoshi, determined to stamp out the growing influence of Catholicism, which he saw as a weapon of Western political power, ordered the arrest in Kyoto and Osaka of six Jesuit missionaries and 20 Japanese Christian converts, including three young boys. He had them executed by crucifixion in Nagasaki as an exemplary lesson in the heartland of the country's Catholicism. The martyrs were canonized in 1862 and their statues erected on the site of their crucifixion 100 years later. A small **museum** displays *krishitan* relics, including a communion wafer that has survived in dehydrated form from the 17th century. The museum relates how other Christians were boiled alive in 1615 at the nearby Unzen hot springs. (But it should not be forgotten that equally cruel religious persecution—of Protestants, Catholics and Jews—was not unknown in the Europe of those times.)

Flowers add an intimate dimension to the massive peace monument.

Peace Park (at Hamaguchi-machi, north-west of Nagasaki Station) covers the site of the atom bomb's epicentre. According to official figures, the bomb left 73,884 dead, 74,904 injured and 71,585 unscathed. On a much smaller scale than the memorial park in Hiroshima, the park has a monumental sculpture by local artist Kitamura Seibo, which stirred considerable controversy when unveiled in 1955. The massive naked meditating figure points a warning right hand skyward and stretches out his left hand in apparent reconciliation. Several other symbolic statues have been donated from around the world, none more eloquent than the simple *Mother and Child* from Nagasaki's sister city of Middelburg, in the Netherlands. Again, as in Hiroshima, the most moving "monument" is the one piece of masonry left standing, in this case the red-brick and grey-stone remains of an arch of the Urakami Catholic Church, at the time the largest in the Orient. From the third floor of the Peace Museum, you get a good view of the imposing new Urakami Church.

At the end of the day, take the cable car to the top of the 1,089-foot (332-m.)-high **Mt. Inasa** across the bay for a sunset view of the city and harbour as the lights begin to twinkle on. Nagasaki is at peace again.

NORTHERN HONSHU AND HOKKAIDO

The regions north-east of Tokyo are more sparsely inhabited and less often visited by tourists, Japanese or foreign. But both northern Honshu, more commonly known as Tohoku, and the northernmost island of Hokkaido have at the same time the advantage of unspoiled countryside and friendly down-to-earth villagers still imbued with something of a frontier spirit. Their folkcrafts are authentic and much less commercialized than elsewhere in Japan and their festivals—in an area without sophisticated entertainments—frequent, colourful and more spontaneous in atmosphere than in the more densely populated regions of the country. Anyone attempting an overall view of Japanese life should certainly pay at least a short visit to these northern territories.

Tohoku

Until the Tokugawa shoguns completed their conquest of the whole of modern Japan from the 17th century on, the towns of Tohoku constituted the northern boundaries of the Japanese empire. Beyond them were the tribes of the Ainu, who were not then considered Japanese. It was only when the Ainu were progressively driven north up into Hokkaido that Tohoku was opened up to broader settlement.

Its extraordinarily rich rice-yield has made Tohoku the chief supplier of the country's needs—still 20 per cent of the national rice crop—and so the general trend of more and more peasants drifting away from the land to the cities has been less marked here. (The perennial bumper rice crops also produce some of the best *sake* in the country.)

The very remoteness of Tohoku was appealing to religious sects such as the Zen Buddhists, espousing an ascetic, unworldly life and constructing here some of the country's finest Buddhist temples. During the Tokugawa shogunate, architecture and sculpture were promoted by the powerful Date clan who ran their fiefdom from the castle-town (and now prefectural capital) of Sendai.

Sendai itself, practically wiped out in World War II and rebuilt as a bright and bustling town with an international university, is best used as a gateway—on the *shinkansen* line—to the region's important sightseeing destinations.

Matsushima is treated by the Japanese with almost holy awe as one of the country's Three Great Scenic Beauties. (This is part of the Japanese passion for cataloguing things in three of this or eight of that.) The other two Great Scenic Beauties, acknowledged for centuries and not some recent public relations gimmick, are Miyajima, with its *torii*-in-the-sea (see p. 151), and Amano-hashidate, a long pine-covered promontory on Miyazu Bay north of Kyoto.

You can get to Matsushima in 40 minutes by train from Sendai, but the nicest way is to stop off en route at Shiogama and take the one-hour boat cruise across Matsushima Bay. The undeniable Scenic Beauty is created by the scores of tiny islands dotting the bay, their white sandstone shaped by the elements into arches, caves and pyramids and covered with lovely wispy sea-pines. The total effect of the changing perspectives as you cruise slowly past is quite extraordinary.

In the town of Matsushima, visit the pretty **Kanrantei Pavilion** for one of the best views of the bay from a rocky cliff beside the landing stage for the cruise ships. But practically any point on the hills that rise behind the town offers a spectacular view.

Zuiganji Temple is the centre of an old Zen Buddhist seminary, its present buildings constructed by the lord of Tohoku, Masamune Date, in 1609. In the temple's Treasure House, you can see a masterly statue of the crusty old warlord in all his armour. He lost his right eye—from smallpox, not in battle—and was nicknamed *Dokuganryu*, "One-Eyed Dragon". The Treasure House also boasts some fine screen-paintings by artists of the Kano school.

As you walk up the long cedar-shaded avenue to the temple, notice the two-storey caves hewn from the rock and serving as accommodation for itinerant monks.

The town of **Hiraizumi** (20 minutes' bus ride from Ichinoseki Station on the Tohoku *shinkansen*) is important for two temples of the late Heian period (early 12th century). **Chusonji Temple** was built by the once mighty Fujiwara family when their power behind the throne in Kyoto was waning—but not their private fortune. Two structures have survived the countless wars of the Fujiwara. The **Konjikido**

(Golden Hall) is a fabulously rich mausoleum which Kiyohira Fujiwara built for himself in 1124. Everything—the doors, bells, Buddha sculptures, pillars and roof beams—are coated in pure gold; everything except the uppermost roof-covering that originally faced the elements. Originally, because this priceless treasure (believed to be what Christopher Columbus was after in his search for the country he called Chipangu) is now protected by glass inside a fireproof concrete Kamakura-style hall.

The **Kyozo** is even older (1108) and used to house the temple's Buddhist *sutras* (scriptures),

Modern artists keep Buddhist art alive at Zuiganji Temple.

The First Japanese

The Ainu, it is now generally accepted, constituted the aboriginal population of the Japanese islands. Anthropologists see in them physical similarity—sloping foreheads, deeply sunken eyes and broad noses—to certain peoples of Russian Siberia, while linguists have related Ainu vocabulary and grammar to South-East Asia and even Aborigine Australia. These are not incompatible, since the Japanese islands were probably settled from both the North and South Pacific before migrants arrived from China and Korea.

Because of their abundant body hair and full beards, the Ainu were for centuries known to the Japanese majority as mishikase or "hairy people", alien to the otherwise homogeneous Japanese community. Today, in a modern society beset by problems of ecology, many Japanese have discovered a new interest in the Ainu, with their close attachment to nature, their knowledge of medicinal plants and herbs and their continued worship of the animals they used to hunt and live with—bear, wolf, eagle and owl.

Once markedly different from other Japanese in appearance—dressing in long coats of woven elm-bark fibres, while marriageable women used to tattoo what was considered an inviting ring around their lips—assimilation to mainstream Japanese society is now almost complete. Decimated over the centuries by disease and persecution, the number of Japanese identifying themselves as Ainu today is not more than about 24,000, practically all descendants of mixed marriages, while the total unmixed population is estimated at less than 200.

which are now kept in the modern Sankozo Treasure House. Other relics of the Fujiwara family on show in the Treasure House are some handsome giltwood coffins and a splendid bronze temple-gong decorated with peacocks.

Hiraizumi's other reminder of the golden days of the Heian era is the grand ruin of the **Motsuji Temple** (founded in 850), still worth visiting for the classical Heian *jodo* (paradise) garden, itself not at all manicured, but all the more charming for that. The large central Oizumigaike Pond, with its islands around which the Fujiwara nobles took cruises in dragon-headed canoes (nice copy lies half-sunken at the edge), is pure fairyland.

Nature sculpts its own statues in the rocks dotting Matsushima Bay.

Hokkaido

This is Japan's Far North. Opened up to full-scale settlement only after the Meiji Restoration of 1868, Hokkaido is still a community of pioneering souls. Here are some of the few Japanese who can still benefit from uncrowded cities, enjoy the unspoiled wilderness, and pursue a simpler existence in a climate and landscape comparable to Scandinavia —snowcapped mountains and pine forest, becoming subarctic in its northernmost area.

The island's capital, Sapporo, was a natural choice for Japan's first staging of the Winter Olympics, in 1972, but in summer the mountains and lake country are mild enough for good camping and hiking.

It was perhaps appropriate that the people the Meiji government chose at the end of the 19th century to "colonize" Hokkaido were the bands of samurai who could not find employment in the new administration, commerce and industries that sprang up with the dismantling of the feudal system. These sturdy men, adventurous but still attached to the old traditions, took their families to Hokkaido to carve out a new life for themselves without having to face too much modern life too quickly. They can be compared to the Americans who were moving to the Far West round about the same time

and, in this century, up to Alaska. Indeed, American advisers helped develop Hokkaido's agriculture and coal mining and lay out an urban grid-system for Sapporo.

If the analogy of the American pioneers is valid for the vast majority of Hokkaidans, then the tiny, but historically significant Ainu community can be compared to the American Indians or Eskimos, both in their

182

folk traditions and in their relationship to the central government. After years of neglect and discrimination, the Japanese government, says a major Japanese encyclopaedia, "is showing a growing concern not only to preserve but to learn from Ainu culture". As a result, Hokkaido has some fascinating museums devoted to Ainu life, and the village of Shiraoi preserves the artefacts and folkcrafts of their culture.

Until skiing starts, Hokkaido's mountains belong to the cranes.

Sapporo

One of the most attractive postwar urban innovations in Japan is Sapporo's **Odori Promenade**, a broad green boulevard lined with flower beds, lilac and maples and with fountains down the middle, running east-west for a straight mile. Street-vendors in the park sell tasty snacks and you can enjoy a people-watching picnic on the grass in the very heart of the city, a great place to start.

Susukino is Sapporo's Ginza, a shopping centre underground—absolutely essential in this northern climate's winter, with covered arcades that slide back their roofs in summer—and a bouncing entertainment district at street level. The town may not be sophisticated, but it has great *joie de vivre*.

Sapporo is nationally famous for its beer (introduced in the 1870s by a German brewer who recognized the surrounding country's hop-growing potential). The **Beer Garden**, north-east of the downtown area, is a lusty place to sample the town's frontier spirit.

Founded only in 1869, with just seven settlers and a few longer-established Ainu families, the town cherishes its rare old-fashioned buildings. The Hokkaido Prefectural Government Building looks like a Victorian red-brick town hall, with a venerable council chamber where the public can see portraits of their founding fathers. The town's oldest building (1878), the **Clock Tower** is now a municipal library. As the English inscription says: "The Tower Bell has been ringing on the hour since 1882, and even today its nostalgic dong plays poetry to Sapporo people".

The **Historical Museum of Hokkaido** recounts the official history of the island's Ainu community and the Meiji pioneering days. Russian sleighs left by traders from Sakhalin Island show that the Americans were not Hokkaido's only advisers.

The **Batchelor Museum** in the Botanical Gardens has a more intimate collection of Ainu artefacts, assembled by British missionary John Batchelor, one of the first scholars to study the life of the Ainu people. The intriguing display includes an "envelope" of bamboo straw serving as a baby's coffin, a flute used to decoy deer and a "libation wand" with a moustache-lifter, which the "hairy" Ainu used when drinking a rice-wine libation to their gods.

Around the Island
Toyako Spa—yes, there are hot springs up north, too—has a beautiful setting on Lake Toya in the mountains south of Sapporo. Take an early morning cruise on the lake and on a summer evening watch the nightly fireworks display, with rockets dropped by motor boats shooting out of the water—very spectacular.

What must be described as the nicest little volcano in Japan is

Mt. Showa-Shinzan, (a 15-minute bus ride from Toyako), "the only privately owned volcano in the world", as owner Mr. Saburo Mimatsu puts it. His late stepfather acquired the volcano when it erupted out of his wheatfield on a sunny June day in 1945. The Japanese government would like to buy the volcano, but the family won't sell. A small museum tells the story and sells souvenir postcards of the old man's paintings of his wheatfield before and after.

Lake Shikotsu, a volcanic crater-lake is one of the most picturesque camping and hiking areas in southern Hokkaido, 16 miles (26 km.) west of Chitose, the island's main airport. There's great salmon fishing from May on.

Shiraoi (30-minute train ride from the spa town of Noboribetsu) is a well-reconstructed Ainu village with Ainu artisans demonstrating their traditional arts and crafts. But best of all is the superb **Ainu Museum**, mounted with the help of European and American anthropologists, setting out Ainu history in a clear and very moving exhibition. The museum has taken the place of the *koyo* or traditional Ainu story-teller, who, in the absence of a written language, perpetuated his people's culture by verbally passing on the folklore to the next generation.

WHAT TO DO

Sports

When the Japanese decide to do something, they seem to go about it with much more enthusiasm and dedication than Westerners usually muster. Take, for instance, the workers doing their calisthenics or communal rope-skipping in the factory courtyard before heading for the conveyor belt. And it is not unusual to see a Japanese golfer-businessman (priority not always clear) standing by himself on a secluded part of the railway platform quietly practising his putting or driving action with an imaginary club. Drivers on tour buses can't wait for their passengers to leave the car park so that they can get out the club they've brought with them, find a patch of grass and bash a dozen imaginary balls into the blue yonder. Practice driving nets are set up on the roofs of apartment and office buildings all over the cities.

Participant Sports

You may find the big city **tennis** courts are crowded, so your best bet is at the seaside or hot spring resorts. Get your hotel to advise you on how to make reservations where necessary.

Golf, on the other hand, is prohibitively expensive and you have to share the Japanese golfer's manic obsession to want to shell out green fees of up to 20,000 yen at peak periods of the year. Unless, of course, you have a business connection paving the way for you, in which case you'll enjoy courses such as the Phoenix and municipal courses in Myajima (Kyushu) or other resorts.

Swimming is a crowded proposition at the beaches close to Tokyo and Osaka (except after September 1, when summer for the Japanese has officially ended). So you're better off going south to Kyushu, around Shimabara and the more secluded of the Amakusa Islands (good scuba-diving and snorkelling, too) or to the spa resort of Ibusuki. **Water sports** fanatics go south to the beaches of Okinawa, the liveliest being Moon Beach at Nakadomari.

One of the joys of **fishing** in Japan is taking the catch back to your Japanese-style inn, *ryokan* or *minshuku*, and having the cook grill it for you or turn it into *sushi* or *sashimi*. Freshwater angling—for bass, carp or trout—is good anywhere in the mountain lakes and streams, best of all up in Hokkaido where you stand a decent chance of hooking a salmon. Sea bream and sea bass are the most frequent catch in coastal waters. Ask the local TIC about licence restrictions.

Skiing is popular on Mt. Zao and at Teine Olympia (outside Sapporo) in Hokkaido, and at Sugadaira and Shiga Heights (Joshin-etsu Kogen National Park) in the Japan Alps.

Spectator Sports

These offer another great opportunity for gaining an insight into the famous Japanese psyche.

To start with the modern, **baseball** is at least as popular in Japan as in the United States. It was introduced back in the 19th century, along with the railway, cameras and whisky. Today it's big business, with cheerleaders, balloons and Nippon variations on the Yankee razzmatazz. The major professional teams are owned by the biggest publishing empires or department store chains, each combining their company name with the time-honoured American sobriquets, the most famous being the Yomiuri Giants. Japanese commentators have happily adopted the American jargon of "strike one", "ball two", "home run" and "pinch hit". In Tokyo, you can see games at Korakuen Stadium, in Osaka at Nissei.

Of the Japanese traditional sports, **sumo wrestling** is far and away the most popular. This ancient, highly ritualized sport goes back 15 centuries and more to Shinto religious ceremonies, when contests were held at the harvest festivals. Today, the

For the Japanese, golf acquires an almost religious mystique.

sumo champions—the only men still allowed to wear the samurai warrior's gleaming top-knot hairdo—are national heroes much in demand for television commercials. At the national level, there are 575 wrestlers classed in six divisions according to their win-loss ratio in the six

187

annual 15-day tournaments. The highest division is the *makuuchi*, of which the champions are known as *yokozuna*. The towering giants weigh anything from 200 to 350 pounds (90 to 165 kg.), yet have an unmistakable grace and dignity if you should ever see them walking in the street.

The *dohyo-iri* (ring entry) ceremony opening the tournament is quite simply awesome. The champions strut into the arena in richly embroidered silk "aprons" covering the solid band protecting their genitals. In the *dohyo*, a ring of hard clay 15 feet (4.6 m.) in diameter under a canopy shaped like a Shinto roof, they

Staring each other down is more than half the business of sumo.

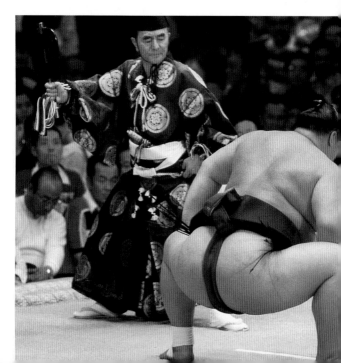

rinse their mouths with "power water", toss salt across the *dohyo* to purify it of evil spirits, swagger around and prepare the all-important "psyching-out" of the opponent. Alternately scowling or disdainfully refusing to look at each other, they flex their muscles and then squat down and stamp into the classic stance of equilibrium. Squaring off like this can take up to five minutes (it was once unlimited), stopping and starting again, all part of the ritual build-up of tension before the wrestlers are obliged finally to clash.

The aim of the match is for one wrestler to force the other out of the ring or to make him touch the floor with any part of the body but the bottom of the feet; there are 70 classified holds and manoeuvres with which to achieve this. The bout is usually over in one or two minutes, but the intensity of the struggle quickly wins over the uninitiated spectator to passionate participation in the general excitement.

Tournaments are held January, May and September at the Kuramae Kokugikan in Tokyo, March in Osaka, July in Nagoya and November in Fukuoka (Kyushu).

Most major cities have **martial arts** halls in which you can watch *kendo*, fencing with bamboo staves as well as the internationally famed sport of *judo,* and *aikido*. The last is a highly spiritual art in which, unlike judo, the opponents do not hold each other at the beginning of the bout, preferring to manoeuvre and feint around each other, applying the strength of their will, *ki*, rather than physical strength to overcome the other. They exploit, for example, the attacker's own momentum and strength to force him off balance.

Looking High and Low for Geishas

Few aspects of Japanese life are more elusive than the authentic geisha. You may see cheap imitations in expensive nightclubs on Tokyo's Ginza or even a real one being driven past in a limousine to some party in the Pontocho or Gion district of Kyoto. But as a non-Japanese, you are unlikely to see an honest-to-goodness geisha girl actually performing (for that is what she is, a performer) unless you yourself are the guest of a Japanese businessman with a very fat expense account. An evening with authentic geisha girls costs a great deal of money and it is, to all intents and purposes, unheard of for them to perform for unescorted foreigners, who are just not considered sufficiently versed in Japanese custom to appreciate the finer points of this time-honoured institution.

The word *geisha* means "talented person"—in Kyoto, as befits the old imperial capital, she's more elegantly known as *geiko*, "talented lady". She has the sophisticated talents of a singer, dancer, actress and musician, well versed in traditional instruments such as the three-stringed *shamisen*. A girl is taken on in her teens as an apprentice, *maiko*, and given a careful training by older geisha girls in the gentle arts of entertaining Japanese gentlemen who want a traditional evening off in an elegant teahouse, away from their wives. With an elaborate hairdo and white face make-up in the style of the Kyoto court lady and dressed in finest kimono, she will sing, dance, recite and play for her high-paying guest, chat and prepare ceremonial tea or occasionally something stronger.

Contrary to popular conception, a geisha is not a glorified prostitute. A genuine geisha has in Japan the prestige and admiration accorded to actresses or singers at the top of their profession in the West. Charm and personality are considered more important than physical beauty.

The risqué reputation derives from the pseudo-geisha girls known as *makura geisha*, literally "pillow geishas", enlisted for hotel stag-parties. They dress in traditional kimono, minus the hallowed white make-up, perform, usually inadequately, the same songs and dances as the geisha, with whisky or *sake* replacing the tea, and then pair off with the party guests.

What you are most likely to come across are very distant cousins of the geisha, the girls in the *kara oke* bars, to which a visit is heartily recommended. Meaning literally "without orchestra", these small bars can be found in the entertainment districts where tired businessmen go to unwind in the congenial but respectable company of a *hosutessu* who chats amiably and keeps their whisky glass or *sake* cup full to the brim. Taped music of popular songs, Japanese or Western, is played non-stop, and every now and again one of the clients goes up to a microphone on the

small spot-lighted stage and, solo or in a duet with his *hosutessu*, sings his favourite song. Amazing how well some of these businessmen can sing and how uninhibited the bad ones are. As a foreigner you will be a big hit if you volunteer—they weep at Paul McCartney's *Yesterday* and it'll make a change from the umpteenth Japanese version of Frank Sinatra's *I Did it My Way*, particularly popular with top Tokyo executives. These sessions go on late into the night until your Japanese hosts—it's more fun if you can get someone to take you—head rather tipsily home to their wives. While the Japanese only rarely go to the *kara oke* in couples, it's graciously accepted for Westerners to do so, though unaccompanied ladies will probably not find a table available. There are thousands of these bars all over Japan—in Tokyo, mostly around the Ginza, Shinjuku, Akasaka and Roppongi.

Entertainment

Theatre in Japan is an adventure all in itself. Traditional Japanese drama, because of its stylization, extravagant gesture and sometimes solemn intonation, may sometimes be difficult for Westerners to appreciate at first look, but it more than repays persevering for a while to get used to the conventions. The growing impact of the impassioned performances, aided by superb costumes and elaborate make-up and masks, can be infectiously exciting, and many a sceptic has come out an addict. Most Japanese theatre aims less at developing a coherent plot, in the Western manner, than at creating a particular tone, atmosphere and strong emotion.

Noh drama is the oldest theatrical form, properly speaking, and the most austere and demanding. Derived from the ritual *sangaku* dances of the court at Nara and Kyoto, it became in the 14th century a fully developed drama of chanting, dancing and highly stylized acting.

A hero and just two or three supporting actors perform themes on the gods, historic battles, ghosts, unhappy love, grief-stricken insanity. The more solemn themes alternate with *Kyogen* farces about the life of the common people, which have a light satirical touch. The commentary is chanted by a chorus of six to eight narrators, reminiscent of the chorus in Greek tragedy, who sit at the side of the stage, while musicians against the stage's back wall provide the sparse accompaniment with flute and drums. Contrasting with the resplendent costumes, the set has an austere simplicity—a backdrop (actually a permanent wall) of a large pine tree and some bamboo, no curtain. The stage is canopied by a classical Japanese tiled roof making a "house" inside the theatre.

Males play all the roles, adult actors play children, while youngsters are sometimes called upon to play an emperor (so as not to upstage the socially less exalted hero).

Performances last several hours, with as many as five plays in one programme. You can probably manage at least a couple—the theatres provide a good buffet between plays. See the best at Tokyo's National Noh Theatre, Kanze Kaikan at Shibuya or the Kyoto National Noh Theatre. Other fine troupes perform in Osaka and Kanazawa.

Ever since the Tokugawa shoguns restricted performances to the samurai classes, *noh* drama has had a rather elitist appeal.

Splendid costumes and masks are an important part of noh *theatre.*

Kabuki has proved much more popular. Just as stylized in its way, *kabuki* is filled with fantastic colour, movement, action, high drama and low comedy.

The actors are folk heroes, and the greatest of them, descendants of centuries-old dynasties of actors, are declared "Living National Treasures", the titular equivalent of the distinction bestowed on the country's great temples, palaces and other artistic masterpieces. Audience participation is at fever-pitch, with people crying out as their heroes enter: "This is what we've been waiting for!" or "You're the greatest in Japan!"

Nothing is spared in the way of gorgeous costumes and decor. Since the 18th century they've used revolving stages and trapdoors through which supernatural characters rise to the stage. Popular, but art of the highest order, *kabuki* tells stories of horror, blood and thunder, passionate love, heroic sacrifice. Connoisseurs wait for the set pieces: the colourful parade of the courtesan, a poignant *seppuku* suicide, the exciting but exquisitely choreographed fight scenes, and—summit of the art of *kabuki*—the end of a love affair that the heroine must break off, perhaps to save her lover's honour, but never because she no longer loves him. A good performance of this moment, with pathos-laden music to pinpoint the excruciating suffering behind her apparently harsh words, will be received as boisterously as a baseball home-run by the Yomiuri Giants.

"She" is in fact likely to be a 60-year-old man. In the early days of *kabuki*, at the beginning of the 17th century, prostitutes usually played the female roles and so the prudish shogun Tokugawa banned all female performers. He then found that the young men who took over the female roles were encouraging homosexuality in their overly erotic love scenes. So they were in turn replaced by older men. After years

of study, these *onnagata*, female impersonators, make an astoundingly subtle and delicate art of capturing the gestures and movements of young girls or old crones.

At Tokyo's Kabukiza Theatre (Higashi-Ginza subway station), you can rent English-language earphone-guides which provide simultaneous translation of all the important dialogue, along with first-class explanations of the action and *kabuki* conventions. Shows, comprising several pieces, last up to four hours, but you can buy cheaper balcony tickets for just a part of the programme. Kyoto's *kabuki* troupe

performs in December and Osaka's in May.

Bunraku, Osaka's famous Puppet Theatre can be seen at the Asahi-Za, but performances are also put on several weeks in the year at Tokyo's National Theatre (Nagatacho subway station). This is theatre for adults more than for children, using the same dramatic themes, stories and conventions as *noh* and *kabuki*, but achieving a unique im-

Disco-dancing in Harajuku is as stylized as classical theatre.

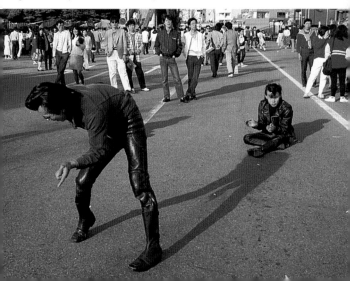

pact with the almost life-size, colourfully costumed puppets. One of the fascinating aspects of *bunraku* is how the puppet-handlers, dressed all in black, are visible on stage manipulating and walking around with their puppets, yet quickly "disappear" from your perception as the magic of the puppets' drama takes over.

Bunraku's heyday was the beginning of the 18th century when playwright Monzaemon Chikamatsu wrote works specially for the puppets (and since often adapted for *kabuki*), which are regarded as among the greatest achievements of Japanese literature. Heroism in battle and the noble values of the samurai tradition are the principal themes of *bunraku* drama. It comes as quite a shock to watch a warrior performing his final gesture of *seppuku* suicide and realize that it's only a puppet. The emotional effect is horrifyingly undiminished.

Theatre that will be more familiar to Westerners (though without translation-aids, so go with a Japanese friend) is also available. But here, too, you will recognize the stylistic influences of traditional drama. **Shimpa** is the sentimental melodrama that began in Japan's "Victorian" age of the Meiji Restoration. **Shingeki** offers more realistic drama of foreign inspiration, including Japanese versions of Shaw,

Ibsen and O'Neill, particularly interesting if you know the originals and want to compare styles.

Film buffs may want to sample Japan's renowned cinema on its home ground. It is, of course, much more—or much less—than the artistic fare of the great directors Kurosawa, Ozu, Imamura and Oshima, though these are still to be seen, along with the newer talents of Kawashima and Imazeki. The samurai epics have moved over to daytime television as unending serials, but most popular are good clean romantic stories for all the family, rather soppy stuff in which the lovers don't so much as kiss.

If you'd like to see how the Japanese handle Western **popular music** and **dancing,** you'll find good quality jazz clubs, conventional discos with, naturally, fantastic electronic equipment, and even country and western saloons, all in Tokyo's cosmopolitan restaurant districts of Akasaka and Roppongi. Teenagers might like to join the open-air disco hordes at Harajuku, near Yoyogi Park.

For information on all current Tokyo theatre programmes and show times, consult the free weekly magazines *Tour Companion* and *Weekender* available in your hotel. And follow the up-to-date reviews in the arts section of the English-language dailies, also free at your hotel.

Festivals and Folklore

In a country with such a highly developed sense of ritual, festivals are a whole way of life. The Japanese love them. You seem to bump into one every other week all over the country. Each region has its own particular festivals or variations on the big ones celebrated nationally, usually dedicated to Shinto deities and shrines or to the major Buddhist temples. The centrepiece of the processions is often a bunch of half-naked youths with white sweat bands around their heads hauling a "portable" shrine through the streets, followed by colourful floats.

Festivals are where the old and new Japan come together, where the ancient traditions are upheld, particularly in remote rural districts, but also where the prosperous new consumer spirit in the big cities adds an inevitable commercial touch to the celebrations.

January. New Year's Day is *the* big Japanese festival, closest in spirit to Christmas in the West, the time when relatives and friends pay visits to each other and to the local shrines. The festive meal of *toshi-koshi soba* buckwheat noodles, extra long for an extra long life, and rather heavy *mochi* rice dumplings, is washed down with plenty of *sake*. (New Year's Eve is a much quieter, more solemn affair than in the West.) Houses, shops and offices are decorated with a bouquet of pine and bamboo, symbols of evergreen stability and upright behaviour. In Tokyo on January 2, the inner grounds of the Imperial Palace are opened to the public and thousands flock in to pay their respects to the emperor—and take a closer peek at his palace than they get the rest of the year.

February. If you're around Okayama on the third Saturday in February, don't miss the astounding spectacle of the Naked Festival at Saidaiji Temple. Thousands of men wearing only a loincloth pack into the main sanctuary to fight for the lucky *shingi* deity-symbol, which a priest flings to them at 2 o'clock in the morning.

Up in Hokkaido, at Sapporo, is the great Snow Festival (1st or 2nd week of February). Its highlight is a competition of ice sculpture at Odori Park, with spectacular models of feudal castles and giant samurai warriors.

March. The three-week Torch Festival of chanting *sutra* scriptures, clanging bells, blowing conch shells and banging iron staves at Nara's Todaiji Temple reaches its climax in the night of March 12th to 13th. At midnight, the 7-foot (2-m.)-high torches are lit and waved about by 12 young novices doing acrobatic dances. They send showers of sparks over the crowd of onlookers, who protect their heads with umbrellas while trying to catch a flake of fire as a lucky charm.

April. Best place to view the spring azaleas is at the Azalea Festival at Tokyo's Nezu Shrine in the last week of April. They have 3,000 bushes there.

May. The nationwide Boys' Day (May 5) is now officially called Children's Day to include the girls, but the emancipated view is taking a long time to catch on. This festival is celebrated with giant paper *koi-nobori* carp flying from poles all over the countryside. The carp's ability to struggle upstream against a strong current is regarded as a fit model for Japanese boys.

On May 15, Kyoto celebrates its big *Aoi Matsuri* Hollyhock Festival. This ancient ritual is meant to prepare for good harvests with branches of hollyhock to stave off thunder and earthquakes. The hollyhock decorates a big red oxcart accompanied from the Imperial Gosho Palace by 300 Kyoto citizens splendidly dressed in Heian-period costumes. Also in Kyoto, on the third Sunday in May, there's a Boat Festival at Arashiyama, where the *yakata* boats, decorated with red and black awnings and dragon heads on their bows, carry musicians, dancers and poets down the Hozu River.

July. Kyoto's *Gion* Festival, from the 17th to the 24th, is the most elaborate procession of the year, with grandiose floats and glowing lanterns. Originally, the festival invoked the gods' help against a plague in medieval Kyoto, but imitations of it, highly commercialized, are now celebrated all over the country.

Immediately after Gion, on July 24 and 25, Osaka holds its mammoth *Tenjin Matsuri* start-

Preparing for purification at Kyoto's Hollyhock Festival.

ing from the Temmangu Shrine, with fireworks, flaming torches, gaily decorated floats on the Yodo River. This is where you can see the lusty young manhood of Osaka go beserk with the festive spirit as they struggle with the huge portable shrine to the river.

August. At the height of summer, variously in July or August, a national Festival of the Dead is celebrated in deliberately colourful and joyous fashion to comfort the spirits of the dead. At Nagasaki in mid-August glowing lanterns decorate the graveyards while other lanterns are put out to sea on model boats to take the departed souls back to their other world.

Shopping

The Japan of the modern era has happily embraced the consumer society and shopping can be a full-time pursuit, to the exclusion of all other activities. The Japanese themselves, in the big cities at least, are to be seen more often than not with some kind of shopping bag—they make very large, sturdy ones—just on the off chance that they might want to buy something. You cannot get to know this country properly, even if you don't want to buy anything, without browsing around the tasteful products of traditional arts and crafts, the great modern cornucopia of electronic gadgets and precision instruments, or the just as impressive ghastly rubbish of the souvenir shops in the major tourist centres. Shopping in Japan takes on the dimensions of an anthropological expedition.

But, for the foreign visitor, some important general advice: Japan is prosperous and not cheap, so don't expect fabulous bargains. The country has succeeded economically by fixing the best price it can get for everything, but the domestic market pays high prices because of a stiff sales tax. What you will pay

Like any party, a Japanese festival is a good excuse to dress up.

in Tokyo is rarely less than the very competitive prices that the exported goods are able to sell at back in your own home town.

While you'll be better off with the staples of Japanese commercial success—cameras, electronics and watches—it's a good idea to start by looking at the range of goods in the department stores and hundreds of speciality shops in the underground shopping centres before going off to find better prices at the discount shops. By the same token, if you're looking for traditional craftwork, go round the local museum first to see what the best of these goods look like. It won't automatically save you from the occasional fake, but at least you'll get a better idea of the authentic stuff before you start hunting for yourself.

Hi-Tech

In Tokyo, the place to go for electronic goods—stereos, radios, calculators—is Akihabara, a whole neighbourhood devoted to multi-floor discount stores selling mountains of electronic equipment at interesting prices. The tax-free department, usually located on the top floor, has more English-speaking sales staff but a narrower range of products. The latest gadgets are not always simultaneously available for the export market. The long-established items may not be greatly different in price from what you might pay in similar stores back home, but the real advantage for the visiting electronics buff is being able to buy the very latest equipment several months before it turns up abroad.

As befits an almost exclusively business-oriented city, Osaka's equivalent discount-shopping neighbourhood, Nipponbashi, specializes in the latest computer equipment, soft- and hardware, with experimental gadgets that are as "state-of-the-art" as you can get outside the laboratories of Silicon Valley.

A word of warning about the electric current. Japan has 100 volts, 50 cycles, slightly different from the United States and completely different from Europe. If you don't want to bother about adaptors (though readily available with the equipment), you should stick to that top-floor tax-free department which specializes in export goods properly adapted for use all over the world.

Cameras. As an exception to the general rule of not making your big purchases before the end of your stay in Japan, it's more logical to buy your camera at the beginning, so that you can try it out during the trip. If there's a fault, you can more conveniently have it repaired or exchanged in Japan than if you only find out about it when you get home. Tokyo's best discount shops are around Shinjuku—almost busy enough to need people-pushers in the shops, too.

Traditional Goods

In this more genteel world, you'll find Japanese **silks** very expensive but of magnificent quality, especially in Kyoto and Kobe. If you can't afford the 500,000 yen that well-to-do ladies pay for their silk kimono, you might like to settle for the more modest, but still very elegant *yukata*, fine cotton kimono, traditionally in indigo-blue and white, at one hundredth the price of the silk. Then you may be able to splash out at least on a silk *obi* sash to tie the *yukata* with added flair. Western-style pyjamas and dressing gowns are to be found in the same materials as the *yukata*. If you're in town for a few days, why not have the garments made, at little extra cost, from the wider range of materials available off the roll.

You can get good-quality copies of colourful *ukiyo-e* woodblock prints which only connoisseurs will distinguish from the originals of the great Edo masters Utamaro and Hiroshige.

Pottery and **ceramics**, both sophisticated and rustic, are an

Takayama's straw-ware is very decorative and a real bargain.

ongoing tradition that has maintained its high standards. Remember to check in the museum before buying in the shops. Kyoto and Kanazawa are major centres. The town of Mashiko, north of Tokyo, is well worth a day's train excursion if you're interested in seeing how some of Japan's most celebrated folkcraft pottery is made, before buying at the workshops at slightly better prices than you'll find back in Tokyo. You can also stay for lessons. (British potter Bernard Leach has had honours showered on him by the emperor for spreading the fame of Mashiko-yaki pottery.) The other internation-

Korean masters shape Kagoshima's famous Satsuma pottery.

Can the Kimono Go West?
If you're a woman, sooner or later the thought's going to cross your mind: "Could I wear a kimono?" If you find yourself attracted to the Japanese style of life, the traditional theatre and the formality of the tea ceremony or ikebana *flower arrangement, the answer may be "yes". Or at least you'll be curious enough to want a closer look at these fascinating garments on display in the department stores (for some reason, nearly always on the fourth floor).*

*There are four basic kinds of women's kimono—*homongi*, the semi-formal patterned silk or satin garment worn for social visits or going to the theatre;* furi-sode*, the unmarried women's formal kimono, more richly patterned and colourful than the* homongi*, often with a layered effect of, say, red over a green undergarment just peeking through to set it off;* tomesode*, the grand black silk kimono with a gold or silver pattern, worn only by married women, for such ceremonial occasions as weddings; and* yukata*, the informal light cotton kimono—for men and for women—that you'll find in your hotel room.*

Special undergarments are worn with the silk kimono—a cotton undershirt and a long sort of underslip cut high at the neck with an interchangeable collar, visible and so matching the kimono. The kimono is tied with the splendid broad obi sash. Wear your hair short or combed up to reveal the nape of the neck, considered the key "glamour-point" of the kimono. A book of kimono etiquette lists 14 different accessories such as the waist pad, a special clip for the obi, white socks with the big toe separate for the thongs of the silk zori sandals, which match the handbag. The whole thing can cost as much as half a million yen. Putting the kimono on takes a minimum of half an hour, during which time you perform 33 different manoeuvres.*

Still interested?

ally known pottery centre is Arita, on the island of Kyushu, not hard to reach from Fukuoka.

You are least likely to go wrong in terms of uniformly high quality if you're in the market for **lacquerware**. Trays, salad and soup bowls and jewellery boxes are superbly finished and not so heavy as to create problems of excess baggage.

Among the many luxury items in Tokyo's antique shops, there are few more breathtakingly exquisite than the **samurai sword**, sharp enough, it is said, to cut a feather in two in midair (or lop a man's head off at one blow). The beauty of its curve and the damascene (fine threads of pure gold or silver beaten into an intricately etched pattern) of the handle somehow transcend its bloodthirsty purpose. Very Japanese, very expensive.

Cloisonné works, beautifully enamelled copper or silver vases and plates in a technique adapted from the Chinese in the 16th century, are also no giveaway in price, but articles of unique craftsmanship. The best quality in damascene and cloisonné products is once again to be found among the old imperial craftsmen of Kyoto. Even without buying, a trip to their workshops is worth the expedition.

Paper goods—fans, dolls and stationery—are more reasonably priced and produced with the same meticulous care as some of those more precious materials.

The Kanda district of Tokyo is devoted almost entirely to **second-hand books**, the biggest neighbourhood of its kind in the world, selling books in most European languages as well as Japanese. You'll also find excellent old maps and prints, but once again the merchants know the going price for everything; real bargains are miracles.

Bargain hunters may have better luck at Tokyo's **flea markets.** The most colourful of these is the weekend market at Harajuku. Others are held on alternating Sundays at the various big shrines; details in the daily English-language press.

EATING OUT

The ultimate and most enjoyable adventure into the mysteries of Japanese life may well be the food. The preparation and presentation of Japanese cuisine epitomize the people's eternal attention to form, colour and texture; how the meal looks is at least as important as how it tastes. The bowls and dishes, for

instance, are chosen not to match each other but to suit the food they contain.

Some of the food, raw and cooked, may be strange to the Western palate, but eminently edible, nourishing and, once you've got the hang of it, absolutely delicious.

The secret of enjoyment is to abandon all preconceptions about what a meal should be.

Even if you don't frequent Japanese restaurants back home, you may be surprised at how much of the fare is already familiar to you. And anyway, octopus, grasshoppers and chrysanthemum leaves are just fine when prepared by the right people.

It's nimble work fishing somen noodles out of the trough.

More Than Just a Nice Cuppa

Nothing crystallizes better Japanese formalism and courtesy than the tea ceremony. As you travel around Japan, you'll have the opportunity to participate either in one of the Zen Buddhist temples in Kamakura or Kyoto, or at a teahouse in one of the "strolling" gardens, or even in special rooms at your hotel.

The very first Zen Buddhist monks drank the slightly acrid green tea so as to stay awake while meditating. In the 15th century, Shogun Yoshimasa Ashikaga made a ceremony of tea drinking when he retired from politics to pursue his aesthetic and spiritual preoccupations at his Ginkakuji Silver Pavilion in Kyoto. The elegant ritual was felt to induce the peace of mind necessary to achieve religious enlightenment. A more fiery successor, Hideyoshi, used it to reconcile his samurai warriors with the townspeople after the bitter years of civil war.

Over the centuries, the ceremony has accumulated exquisitely designed utensils—bowls, tea kettle, tea caddy, hot water jug, miniature brazier, a long, slender scoop for the tea powder, and a little whisk for mixing it. As well as the utensils, a painted scroll is hung in an alcove, setting the theme of the occasion, together with a delicate flower arrangement. "Natural" nageire styles or the classically formal rikka arrangements combine three main flower-stems symbolizing man, heaven and earth.

The ceremony usually begins with the serving of moist little manju cakes, which you cut up and eat with tiny wooden picks, or flower-shaped higashi biscuits, while the host prepares the tea. This must be whisked in the caddy to a fine froth with a brisk back and forth motion, weaving round and round. If you are served first, be sure to bow to the host and then turn to your neighbour to say: "Excuse me for drinking before you". Take the bowl with your right hand and rest it on the palm of your left, turning the bowl's decorative pattern away from you, for others to admire. Sip the tea noisily—it's customary—then wipe the bowl's edge and turn its decorative pattern back so as to admire it yourself. It's a very important part of the ceremony to express admiration for the bowls, utensils and other things of beauty in the room. The signal for the end of the ceremony is when the host removes the tea caddy and scoop.

You may be reassured to learn that the first rule of the greatest tea-master of them all, Senno Rikyu, was: "When making a cup of tea to be drunk by a guest, it is more important to make drinkable and pleasant tea than to pay attention to the etiquette of the presentation."

How to Eat

Don't be intimidated by the prospect of arcane rules of etiquette when having your first elegant Japanese dinner. Be aware that different customs may apply, but the Japanese forgive foreigners almost any breach of their etiquette.

Just a few simple tips: taking off your shoes before stepping on the *tatami* mat is no problem, but if you can't kneel on the floor Japanese-style, try any way you're comfortable, with your legs tucked somewhere out of the way, even right under the table. These days, things are made easier with a cushion, an arm rest and even a back support. That marvellous *oshibori* wet towel given you to freshen up at the beginning of the meal should be neatly rolled up when you've finished with it.

And you know already that eating with chopsticks involves moving one of them like a pen while the other stays firm to grip the morsel. If you do it well, don't be surprised when your Japanese friends compliment you profusely. This is not as patronizing as it seems, it's just that proper chopstick-manipulation is a dying art in Japan—the kids have been ruined by fast food and plastic forks.

When drinking *sake*, by all means serve your neighbour, but don't serve yourself, even though you will probably have your own little jug in front of you. Your host is expected—and expects—to do the honours. When eating your soup, take the pieces of food from it with your chopsticks and drink the broth directly from the bowl, as there'll be no spoon. Make all the noise you like, it's expected. Slurping is especially good with noodles, say the Japanese. The extra intake of oxygen is said to improve the taste.

Where to Eat

The high-class places, *ryori-ya* in Tokyo or the provinces, are as expensive as their international reputation, easily the equivalent of top Paris or New York restaurants. Given the meticulous care and delicacy of the ingredients that go into the dinners served there, the prices are not unreasonable, but by and large they remain the preserve of the well-to-do and businessmen on big expense accounts. (This is where you might catch your glimpse of a geisha.) Nevertheless, well-to-do or not, you should think of including in your budget at least one slap-up Japanese dinner with all the trimmings (not necessarily a geisha). You can combine it with your stay at a *ryokan*, where you'll get a great dinner right there in your room. If you prefer an elegant restaurant, besides Tokyo (where abundant tourist-traps for foreigners may make your choice difficult) try one of the great provincial gourmet centres such as Kyoto, Osaka and the major towns of Kyushu. There, you'll be sampling regional delicacies at their freshest.

But Japan is blessed more than most countries with excellent, small, modestly priced restaurants, *koryori-ya*, serving traditional Japanese food of very fine quality. A little smaller than these are the dozens of snack bars, for want of a better word, indicating their speciality by their name, *sushi-ya*, *yakitori-ya*, or *okonomiyaki-ya*.

All of these establishments have a *noren*, a short cloth curtain over the door, as a sign of being open if fluttering outside or closed if tucked inside. Even if you can't read the writing on the sign, you can more often than not tell which kind of place it is by the window display of mind-bogglingly perfect plastic replicas of the meals served inside. These imitations of meat, fish and vegetables, and also of every grain of rice or strand of noodle, are great helps in ordering your meal. If the menu has no explanation in English, just step outside again with the waiter and point to what you want.

Many of these snack bars are located in department stores, alongside the basement food counters, ideal places to take your lunch during your shopping expeditions. If you're really hard up, you can also make a whole meal out of the wonderful

---

Plastic Fantastic

The manufacture of meal replicas is a whole industry in itself that dates back to the Meiji Restoration of 1868, when the Japanese had to explain with models made of wax the new-fangled meals coming in from abroad, for which the Japanese had as yet no name. The factories employ professional cooks to regulate the size, shape and colour of the "food" to be made out of vinyl. It has proved impossible for artisans other than real sushi cooks to compose convincing replicas of the little oblongs of raw fish on rice, but most of the ordinary craftsmen can manage a bowl of noodles all by themselves. Arts students do the painting, and women assemble the finished product on its dish. If you're interested in buying one of these "meals" as a souvenir, they're more expensive than the real thing, but of course last longer. The factories' sales outlets are located in neighbourhoods specializing in restaurant equipment, such as Tokyo's Asakusa. The result is so deceptively right that a sumo wrestler was able to bluff his wedding guests with a complete replica banquet before unveiling the identical thing behind it.

The shrimp are as inviting as the sushi-*man's smile.*

samples offered at the food counters pushing the store's various delicacies-of-the-day.

Lowest on the social rung, but in many ways the most attractive, patronized by rich and poor alike, are the *yatai* pushcarts serving roasted sweet potatoes, dishes of noodles, soup, stew or barbecue, in the street. With a little roof to keep off the rain and often stools for the customers, the vendors set up shop in entertainment districts such as Tokyo's Ginza, Kabuki-cho and Asakusa or around major railway stations like Shibuya or Shimbashi, doing their best business late at night. In rural districts, you can still hear them heralding their arrival with a haunt-

211

ing little tune on a flute as they trundle down the street till stopped by a customer.

So far, this vestige of old Japan has resisted the onslaught of the fast-food chains, but the latter, bearing all the familiar trademarks for hamburger or fried chicken, are as plentiful as in any Western country. Japan's home-grown version of fast food is the neat little *bento* lunch box of traditional rice, fish and vegetable goodies served with a little plastic flask of tea at the railway station or on the train.

In a separate category, *kissaten* are rather sophisticated coffee houses favoured by students, artists and intellectuals, often offering jazz or Western classical music. They serve snacks and, before 10 a.m., a Western-style breakfast for the price of the coffee, a nice change from your hotel dining room.

Deadly Dinner
One adventure to be advised against is a kind of Japanese roulette played with the fugu *blowfish. This allegedly tasty fish, eaten raw as* sashimi, *possesses a lethally poisonous bile which has to be removed by government-licensed experts before the blowfish can be offered to the public. They don't always get rid of all the poison and every year a couple of Japanese thrill-seekers blow it.*

What to Eat

As a general rule you'll notice that the cooked food is served warm rather than hot and the Japanese do not feel it loses its flavour if you let it get cold while sampling something else, since many dishes are served simultaneously. The rice is not cooked till it's dry; it's left, not gooey, but slightly sticky.

Breakfast Japanese-style may not be your cup of tea every day, but try it at least once, and if you do stay in a *ryokan* or *minshuku*, you should know what to expect. The full meal is likely to include some cold fish, raw or pickled, hot *miso-shiru* soup with a few vegetables and *tofu*, white soya bean curd, in it (very high protein), a bowl of rice and tea.

Lunch and Dinner. One of the most popular Japanese lunches is buckwheat noodles, *soba*, served with a sprinkling of shredded pork, beef, chicken or egg with leeks and mushrooms in a bowl of fish stock and a *miso* paste of fermented rice or soya bean. One bowl makes more than a meal. There's a spectacular show to be had in watching the cook prepare the noodles from a sheet of dough that he chops up in fine strips at lightning speed with a long straight-edged chopper as sharp as a samurai's sword.

Slightly thicker noodles are known as *udon*, and the yellow curly Chinese variety are *shina-*

soba. The noodles may also be served cold with a dip of soya sauce, fresh chopped onions, ginger and minced radish.

Sashimi, usually served as part of a larger meal, is raw fish sliced in small bite-size pieces of varying shapes. It's dipped in a little sauce, which you prepare to your own degree of spiciness from *wasabi*, mustard-like green horse-radish—a little goes a long way—*shisonomi* herb-buds and soya sauce. Tuna fish is the most common, *maguro* being the deep red meat and *toro* the richer, pink parts. Others are *tai* (sea bream), *tara* (bass), and *aji* (pompano).

Sushi are patties of cold boiled rice with a little diluted vinegar to hold it together in an oblong form and topped by a piece of raw fish, generally making two bites. Besides the *sashimi* fish already mentioned, you will also find pieces of octopus (*tako*), squid (*ika*) and occasionally clams, scallops, abalone, prawn and shrimp, ideally with a little lime juice. Eaten with the same sauce as *sashimi*, the *sushi* needs to be turned upside down so that only the fish is dipped, otherwise the rice-patty disintegrates. In the *sushi* bars, you either sit at a table with a plate of assorted fish and seafood—*ichi-nine-mae* —or else, more fun, up at the counter where you choose the fish you fancy and watch the cook's dexterity as he cuts it up. Beer or hot tea are the things to drink with *sushi*.

Sukiyaki (pronounced *ski-ya-ki*) is perhaps more familiar to Westerners. Indeed, it was introduced in Japan only with the arrival in the 19th century of the Americans who demanded beef. Beginning as a brilliant attempt to imitate, but in fact surpass the sailors' beef-stew, the thin slices of tender filet-cut beef are sautéed before you over a gas or charcoal fire. The meat is stirred with translucent *shirataki* vermicelli, finely shredded leeks, mushrooms and greens—either spinach or, yes, chrysanthemum leaves. All the ingredients are appetizingly set out on a board beforehand. The best meat is the fabled beef of Kobe, where, to give it flavour and keep it tender, the cattle are fed beer and lovingly massaged before slaughter.

For a do-it-yourself meal, try *shabu-shabu*, beef sliced paper-thin, which you boil in a pot set before you with chicken stock, cabbage, carrots, spinach, mushrooms and *tofu* bean curd.

Okonomiyaki is a very cheap do-it-yourself meal, popular with students. It's a Japanese-style pancake which you prepare with a spatula on a hot griddle with an egg batter and pieces of shrimp or meat, as you prefer, and chopped vegetables. A waitress will show you how to do it. Great fun.

If you prefer someone else to do the work for you, *oden* is a lusty variety of hotchpotch, much prized among regulars of the *yatai* street vendors. You'll find everything stewing in the fish broth—cuttle fish, hard-boiled eggs, radish, kelp, seaweed, turnips, rice-dumplings, potatoes and the odd octopus coming up from the lower depths of the cauldron.

Yakitori is quite simply pieces of chicken barbecued on small wooden skewers with onions and green peppers, making a good bar snack with your beer or *sake*.

Tempura is one of the happier Japanese memories of the Portuguese (from a Lenten dish prepared by the missionaries *ad tempora*). Shrimp, prawn, slices of green pepper and other vegetables are coated in a batter of egg and flour, deep fried and dipped in a *ten-tsuyu* sauce of sweet rice-wine, fish broth and soya sauce. *Tempura* is served with a bowl of rice or noodles and a small dish of pickled vegetables on the side.

Besides the vegetables already mentioned and many others familiar in the West, you'll also come across a delightful variety of seaweed, edible roots, grasses, flowers and green twigs that you'd never have dreamed could hop from a vase onto your dinner plate. And taste good.

Having survived such diversions from the culinary beaten track, you might even be ready for some real Japanese exotica. Blue sea slugs, black grasshoppers, lizards, snakes and newts are not just ingredients for Macbeth's three witches, they're perfectly good delicacies to tickle a palate jaded by too much shrimp *tempura*. Your best chance of finding them is in the *ryori-ya* high-class establishment.

Desserts

The Japanese are a little less inventive when it comes to sweets, perhaps because sugar came late to Japan, with the Europeans. But *wagashi*, confectionery from wheat or rice flour, mashed red beans, yams, arrowroot, egg and sugar, is worth a try. The moist sweets are known as *yokan*, a bean-paste jelly served in long rectangles and sliced. *Manju* is a bun stuffed with sweet bean paste, and *senbei* are a kind of cracker. Frequently served at the tea ceremony are the dry *higashi* rice-jellies or biscuits cut in the shape of flowers or leaves.

The Japanese absolutely hated milk when the Americans first suggested getting it from a cow, and the ice-cream has never caught up with Western standards. The one interesting innova-

Nothing staid about Japanese businessmen's picnic-in-the-park.

tion in this domain is *matcha-aisu-kurii-mu,* ice-cream flavoured with green tea.

Drinks

Locally distilled whisky is fast taking over as the preferred strong drink of the middle class, but *sake* remains the national alcohol *par excellence.* It's a colourless wine fermented from rice and usually served warm, but not hot, from clay pots into thimble-size cups—never to be drunk, by the way, while eating rice. Much more potent, Kyushu's *imo-jochu* is a liquor distilled from sweet potatoes, which may be served from a pot made out of a thick hollow bamboo stem.

The Japanese have also produced a very good beer, *biru,* ever since a German visited Hokkaido in the 1880s and found it ideal for growing hops.

And so to tea. The green powdered tea, *cha,* brought originally from China—green because unfermented—is prepared in lukewarm water. *Gyokuro* is the finest quality, used in the tea ceremony. *Sencha* is the most common domestic tea, while *bancha,* the kind served in *sushi* bars and small restaurants, is coarser and needs boiling water. Cheapest of all, the *hoji-cha* served by the street vendors is brown, also brewed in boiling water, with a nice smoky tang to it.

Escape Hatches

You needn't set yourself completely adrift from your normal eating habits—your stomach would probably just not stand for it. Since you may not want to start every day with fish, soup and rice, we recommend you take a Western-style breakfast, have a light lunch of Japanese snacks and go for a whole Japanese meal at dinner time.

If you want a change from Japanese food, you'll find plenty of "foreign" restaurants in the big cities, and the major Western-style hotels have both Western and Japanese menus. Other than steaks, spare-ribs, chops and hamburgers, the most reliable foreign food, as far as quality is concerned, will be found in Asian restaurants—Chinese, Korean, Vietnamese or Indian—where the kitchens are staffed by their nationals, rather than "French", "Italian" or "Viennese" places which all tend to have Japanese cooks. Brilliant but sometimes limited imitators that they are, they'll turn out a *fettuccine alla romana,* a *bœuf bourguignon* or *Sachertorte* that all look absolutely identical to what you're used to, but somehow taste completely different. You also find some strange mixtures of cuisines in the same place —Tokyo has many establishments offering "curry and spaghetti".

Asking the Waiter

The bill (check) please.	お勘定を下さい。	*okanjo, o-negai shimasu*
I'd like a/an/some...	…を一つ/少し	*...o kudasai*
bread	パン	*pan*
coffee	コーヒ・	*kōhi*
fish	さかな	*sakana*
fruit	果物	*kudamono*
pepper	こしょう	*koshō*
potatoes	じゃがいも	*jagaimo*
rice	ごはん	*go-han*
salad	サラダ	*sarada*
salt	塩	*shio*
starter	オードーブル	*ōdōburu*
sugar	砂糖	*satō*
tea	紅茶	*kōcha*
vegetables	野菜	*yasai*
wine	ぶどう酒	*budōshu*

...And Reading the Menu

みそ 味噌	bean paste soup	*miso*
蛤うしお汁	clam soup	*hamaguri ushiojiru*
うなぎ丼	eel with rice	*unagi donburi*
海老ごはん	shrimps with rice	*ebigohan*
よせ鍋	seafood with vegetables	*yosenabe*
天ぷら	deep fried fish and vegetables	*tempura*
豚のしょうが焼き	ginger fried pork	*buta-no-shoga-yaki*
しゃぶしゃぶ	beef steamboat	*shabu-shabu*
すきやき	sliced beef and vegetables	*sukiyaki*
焼きそば	deep-fried noodles	*yaki soba*
豆腐	bean curd	*tofu*
ちまき	rice cakes in bamboo leaves	*chimaki*
ざるそば	chilled wheat noodles	*zaru udon*
焼とり	marinaded skewered chicken	*yakitori*
ごま焼き	sesame chicken	*goma-yaki*
煮物	mixed braised vegetables	*nimono*
焼きなす	baked eggplant	*yaki-nasu*
とんかつ	deep-fried pork fillets	*tonkatsu*
すし	vinegary rice balls with raw fish	*sushi*
さしみ	raw fish	*sashimi*

BERLITZ-INFO

CONTENTS

A ACCOMMODATION

There is a wide range of accommodation to choose from in Japan, from luxury Western-style hotels to Buddhist temples. During the Japanese holidays (see PUBLIC HOLIDAYS) early reservations are essential. If you're stuck without a room, call in at the Japan Travel Bureau (JTB) office (there is one in most towns), where you will be able to find help.

Western-style hotels. Most of the high-standard, Western-style hotels belong to the Japan Hotel Association (JHA):

2-2-1 Otemachi, Chiyoda-ku, Tokyo; tel. (03)3279-2706.

These hotels are comparable to modern hotels in Europe or the United States. They offer conventional Western-style facilities and cuisine, although Japanese food is also available. Rates are on a "per room, per day" basis and can be reduced under certain circumstances (off-season, group discount, long-stay, etc.). Reservations can be made through any travel agent, certain airlines, or by contacting the hotel directly.

Japanese-style inns *(ryokan)*. For a more informal atmosphere, and for a taste of the Japanese way of life, it is an exciting experience to stay in a *ryokan*. These are small, hospitable, family-run hotels, with a minimum of 11 guest rooms.

Reservations can be made through a travel agent. Room prices include breakfast and dinner; the rate is reduced 10–20% if meals are omitted, but this should be decided before you check in. The usual check-in time is between 3 and 4 p.m.; check-out time from 10 to 11 a.m.

Guest houses *(minshuku)* are, like *ryokan,* Japanese-style, and the food is Japanese. They are often located in holiday resorts, and the guest is treated as a member of the family. The overnight charge includes two meals, often featuring regional specialities. The guest is expected to lay out his bedding at night and roll it up and stow it away again the next morning. Reservations can be made by contacting the *minhuku* directly.

Welcome Inn Reservation Centre offers a free reservation service to visitors from abroad at a wide range of *ryokan* and *minshuku*. Reservation request forms are available at JNTO overseas offices and this service is restricted to inns which charge ¥8000 or less per night based on single-room occupancy.

220

Home stay system. Anyone seriously interested in the Japanese way of life can stay with a Japanese family, arranged through the intermediary of the Japanese Association of the Experiment in International Living (EIL Japan) which organizes stays from one to four weeks. Applications should be made to your nearest EIL office six to eight weeks in advance.

P.O. Box 477, Putney, Vermont 05346, U.S.A.; tel. 802/387-4210.

EIL Gt. Britain is at Upper Wyche, Malvern, Worcs. WR14 4EN; tel. 06845/62577.

Buddhist temples *(shukubo)*. If you have a particular interest in Buddhism, you can stay in a Japanese temple and join in the monks' daily life. Food is strictly vegetarian, but well balanced; life is communal and guests are expected to join in with some of the chores. Reservations can be made through the Japan Travel Bureau.

See also CAMPING, YOUTH HOSTELS.

I'd like ...	…が欲しいのですが。	... ga hoshii no desu ga
a single room	シングルルーム	shinguru rūmu
a double room	ダブルルーム	daburu rūmu
a room with bath	風呂付きの部屋	furotsuki no heya
May I see the room?	部屋を見せて頂けますか。	heya o misete itadakemasu ka

AIRPORTS (空港)

Tokyo is the principal gateway to Japan, and practically all international flights land at New Tokyo International Airport (Narita). However, there are also international airports at Osaka, Okinawa and Nagoya, and a limited number of international flights also use Fukuoka, Kagoshima, Niigata, Kumamoto, Nagasaki, Komatsu and Sapporo airports. All airports have modern facilities, including duty-free shops.

New Tokyo International (Narita) is situated some 40 miles (65 km.) east of the city centre. Coaches depart at frequent intervals for the Tokyo City Air Terminal; travel time is approximately 90 minutes. Buy the ticket at the airport arrival hall in front of the customs-area exit. A faster means of transport is the new JR Narita Express train. The station is located under the airport terminal building and the journey to central Tokyo takes 53 minutes. The Keisei Skyliner train is very reasonable in price and only slightly slower on its journey to Keisei Ueno station in Tokyo. A taxi from Narita to the centre of Tokyo takes 60–70 minutes or more, depending on traffic conditions. Inter-airport transfer to Tokyo Haneda Airport by coach takes one hour 40 minutes, and a coach leaves for Yokohama City Air Terminal every 30 minutes (the journey takes about two hours).

N.B. all passengers leaving Tokyo from Narita have to pay an airport tax.

Tokyo International (Haneda) is Tokyo's second airport, 12 miles (20 km.) south of the city centre. Most domestic flights arrive and leave from here. Transport to town is by monorail to Hamamatsu-Cho Station (departure every 6 minutes, travel time 15 minutes).

Osaka International (Itami) is situated 12 miles (20 km.) south-east of the city centre. Coaches depart every 12 minutes for Umeda Bus Station in the centre of Osaka; travel time 30 minutes. City buses to the bus station by the Maru Building leave every 10 minutes and take 30 minutes. Trains run every 15 minutes, and take 20 minutes to reach Hankyu railway station, Umeda. Transfer to Kyoto or Kobe is possible by coach.

Nagoya International (Komaki) is 10 miles (17 km.) from the city. Coaches leave every 15 minutes for Nagoya railway station; the city bus leaves every 30 minutes.

Porter!	ポーター(赤帽)さん。	pōtā san
Can you help me with my luggage?	荷物を運んでください。	nimuotsu o hakonde kudasai
Take these bags to the taxi/bus.	このバッグをタクシー/バスへ持って行ってください。	kono baggu o takushii/basu e motte itte kudasai
How much is that?	いくらですか。	ikura desu ka

C CAMPING (キャンプ)

There is a limited number of camping sites throughout the country. Details can be obtained from the Japan Auto Camping Association:

New Ueno Bldg., 7th floor, 1–24 Yotsuya, Shinjuku-ku, Tokyo.

The Tourist Information Center in Yurakucho can give information about reservations and costs and can supply a map of Japan showing the camping sites. It is possible to camp on private land, but you must first obtain permission from the owner.

Inveterate campers may be interested in staying in public lodgings *(kokumin shukusha)* operated by the Ministry of Health and Welfare, and built in scenic places or national park areas. Lodging includes two meals. Reservations should be made through the Japan Travel Bureau or directly to the lodging.

Government-run *kokumin kyuka mura* are vacation villages, offering recreational facilities. Here too, overnight stay includes two meals. Reservations should be made through the Japan Travel Bureau or through a *kokumin kyuka mura* Service Centre:

Tokyo: 1st floor, Tokyo Kotsu Kaikan, 2-10-1 Yurakucho, Chiyoda-ku.

Osaka: Osaka Station, 3-3-1 Umeda, Kita-ku.

Nagoya: 1st floor, Chunichi Bldg., 4-1-1 Sakae, Naka-ku.

CAR HIRE （レンタカー）

Do not attempt to drive in Japan unless you are really obliged to do so—road conditions are extremely dangerous (see DRIVING). There are car rental firms in all major cities. Except for holders of U.S. and Canadian driving licences, an International Driving Permit is necessary.

It is possible to rent a car with an English-speaking chauffeur, through a hotel or a travel agent.

I'd like a car.	車を借りたいのですが。	kuruma o karitai no desu ga
What's the charge per week?	1週間の料金はいくらですか。	isshu-kan no ryokin wa ikura desu ka
Here's my driving licence.	私の運転免許証です。	watashi no untenmenkyoshō desu

CIGARETTES （タバコ）

The Japan Tobacco Co., Ltd. manufactures 35 different brands of cigarettes, the most popular being filter-tipped low nicotine and tar brands. They can be purchased at tobacconists, magazine stands, coffee shops and from vending machines. Packets bear English names such as *Hi-lite, Cherry* or *Seven Stars.* Imported brands are also available.

Give me a packet of cigarettes, please.	たばこを1箱ください。	tabako o hito-hako kudasai
Have you any matches?	マッチがありますか。	matchi ga arimasu ka

CLIMATE

Japan is situated in the temperate zone of the northern hemisphere and its climate resembles that of Central America or the South of Europe. However, it is difficult to generalize, as the country stretches over 1,860 miles (3,000 km.) and the climate varies according to region and season. Winter temperatures range from −9 °C to +16 °C, summer temperatures from +20 °C to +28 °C. The rainy season lasts from mid-June to the beginning of July. Seven volcanic zones cross the archipelago resulting in occasional earth tremors; typhoons occur frequently.

January and February are the ideal months for winter sports; March, April and May are warm and sunny: cherry blossom and plum blossom time. From mid-June to mid-July is the rainy season, followed by six weeks of hot, jungle-like humidity. September is the month of strong winds, rain and typhoons; followed by clear skies and bright sunshine during the autumn months.

Tokyo temperatures:

		J	F	M	A	M	J	J	A	S	O	N	D
average daily	°F	29	31	36	46	54	63	70	72	66	55	43	33
minimum	°C	−2	−1	2	8	12	17	21	22	19	13	6	1
average daily	°F	47	48	54	63	71	76	83	86	79	69	60	52
maximum	°C	8	9	12	17	22	24	28	30	26	21	16	11

CLOTHING

The Japanese have conservative tastes in clothing: nearly all business-men wear dark suits and impeccable white shirts. Some modesty in dress is therefore required: subdued colouring and subtle design are preferable. Your wardrobe should be versatile, light-weight and easy-to-wash, and should include a raincoat. Extra-warm sweaters and a warm coat are necessary for the winter season. You should avoid tight, restrictive clothing: remember that you will often be seated at low tables with your legs folded underneath you—not easy in a tight skirt. Remember also that your socks will often be on view and you will be embarrassed if your toes poke through holes for all to see; temple floors can be very cold so you should include at least one pair of thick woolly socks. You will have to take your shoes off so often that you will be glad to wear slip-ons. A good stout pair of walking shoes is useful for sight-seeing, as Japanese paths are gravelly and hard.

Should you want to buy clothes in Japan, note that the Japanese have shorter arms and legs than Westerners, and that Japanese underwear does not suit the Western figure.

Women

Dresses/suits						
American	10	12	14	16	18	20
British	32	34	36	38	40	42
Japanese	9	11	13	15	17	19

Stockings						Shoes			
American ⎫ British ⎭	8	8½	9½	9½	10	6 4½	7 5	8 6½	9 7
Japanese	20	21	22	23	24	22	22½	24	24½

Men

Suits/overcoats							Shirts			
American ⎫ British ⎭	36	38	40	42	44	46	15	16	17	18
Japanese	90	95	100	105	110	115	38	41	43	45

Shoes									
American ⎫ British ⎭	5	6	7	8	8½	9	9½	10	11
Japanese	23	24	25	26	26½	27	27½	28	29

COMMUNICATIONS

Post offices. Main post offices open from 8 a.m. to 8 p.m. from Monday to Friday, from 9 a.m. to 5 p.m. on Saturday and from 9 a.m. to noon on Sundays. Branch offices open from 9 a.m.

to 5 p.m. on weekdays, from 9 a.m. to 12.30 p.m. on Saturdays, and are closed on Sundays. Tokyo International Post Office (Tokyo Kokusai Yūbinkyoku, Chiyoda-ku, Otemachi 2-3-3) is open round the clock for urgent mail. Stamps are on sale in post offices, in hotels and from some tobacconists and chemists. Mail boxes (red for domestic mail, blue for overseas mail and express [special delivery]) are placed on street corners. You can also post letters at the hotel desk.

Telephone. Public telephones are differentiated by colour and size; all can be used for local, inter-city or long-distance calls. The yellow and blue phones can be used for reverse-charge (collect) calls, but not the red ones. Green-coloured public telephones marked "International & Domestic Card/Coin Telephone" can be used for direct calls. Cards are available from machines and at telephone offices. However, services like personal (person-to-person) calls, reverse-charge calls and credit calls are not available for every country; you should enquire beforehand. You can also dial direct from KDD (Kokusai Denshin Denwa) offices, which also handle telex, telefax and telegrams. International calls can be booked by dialling 0051 from anywhere in Japan.

Telegrams. Overseas telegrams and faxes can be sent from KDD offices (see above) or from main post offices; you can also ask for help at the hotel desk.

Where's the telephone?	電話はどこにありますか。	denwa wa doko ni arimasu ka
Can you help me get this number?	この番号に電話したいのですけれど掛けて頂けませんか。	kono bangō ni denwa shitai no desu keredo kakete itadakemasen ka
Can I dial direct?	ダイヤル直通ですか。	daiyaru-chokutsū desu ka
What was the cost of that call?	あの電話代はいくらでしたか。	ano denwadai wa ikura deshita ka

CRIME AND THEFT

The crime rate in Japan is extremely low; it is unlikely that you will be attacked or robbed. In Tokyo and other large cities, police boxes are located at most major street junctions, and highway patrols cruise the streets. (See also LOST PROPERTY and POLICE.)

226

CUSTOMS AND ENTRY REGULATIONS

To enter Japan, you will need a valid passport, and you will have to fill in an embarkation/disembarkation card.

Visas. Tourists from the United Kingdom and Ireland do not need a visa if they intend to stay less than 180 days in Japan; Americans, Canadians and New Zealanders can stay 90 days without a visa. Visitors from Australia can obtain a free visa from a Japanese consulate or embassy before leaving home. Any visitor who stays more than 90 days in Japan must apply to the mayor of the city where he is staying for an Alien Registration Certificate. Tourists from South Africa can obtain a visa from a Japanese embassy before leaving. They can stay up to 90 days in Japan.

Customs regulations. The following chart shows the main duty-free items you may take into Japan and, when returning home, into your own country.

Into:	Cigarettes	Cigars	Tobacco	Spirits	Wine
Japan	400 or	100 or	500 g.	3 bottles of ¾ l. each	
Australia	200 or	250 g. or	250 g.	1 l. or	1 l.
Canada	200 and	50 and	900 g.	1.1 l. or	1.1 l.
Eire	200 or	50 or	250 g.	1 l. and	2 l.
N. Zealand	200 or	50 or	250 g.	1.1 l. and	4.5 l.
S. Africa	400 and	50 and	250 g.	1 l. and	2 l.
U.K.	200 or	50 or	250 g.	1 l. and	2 l.
U.S.A.	200 and	100 and	*	1 l. or	1 l.

*A reasonable quantity.

Officially, the goods you import should be declared orally or in writing, but Japan has now adopted the customs clearance system of spot-checking practised in many countries. There are three exits: green (nothing to declare), red (something to declare) and white (for non-residents). There is no limit on the amount of currency you can bring into the country; you can take out up to ¥5 million. If ever you want to take out more, you must obtain permission from the Ministry of Finance.

I have nothing to declare.	申告する物は 何もありません。	shinkoku suru mono wa nani mo arimasen

D DRIVING

Driving in Japan presents several problems, not to be underestimated: traffic keeps to the left, which will not unduly worry British drivers; however, most Westerners will be discouraged by the traffic conditions. The streets are extremely congested and it is forbidden to park or even to stop in some of them. Very few streets have names, and most traffic signs are written in Japanese characters. There are often no pavements (sidewalks) in towns so that pedestrians mingle with the traffic; roads are poorly surfaced and bumpy; telegraph poles are sometimes planted in the middle of the road.

Speed limits are 40 k.p.h. (25 m.p.h.) in towns, 60 k.p.h. (38 m.p.h.) in suburbs, and 100 k.p.h. (63 m.p.h.) on expressways. The Japanese Automobile Federation publishes a *Manual for Drivers and Pedestrians* in English.

E ELECTRIC CURRENT

The current is 100 volts throughout Japan, with 50 cycles in the east and Tokyo, and 60 cycles in western Japan. American-style sockets are used, with flat-pin plugs, so non-Americans will need an international adaptor. However, major hotels have 110 and 220 volt outlets for razors, hair driers, etc.

EMBASSIES

Australia:	1-4, Mita 2-chome, Minato-ku, Tokyo; Tel. (03)5232-4008
Canada:	3-38, Akasaka 7-chome, Minato-ku, Tokyo; Tel. (03)3408-2101
Great Britain:	1, Ichiban-cho, Chiyoda-ku, Tokyo; Tel. (03)3265-5511
New Zealand:	20-40, Kamiyama-cho, Shibuya-ku, Tokyo; Tel. (03)3467-2271
U.S.A.:	10-5, Akasaka 1-chome, Minato-ku, Tokyo; Tel. (03)3224-5172

EMERGENCIES (緊急時) (see also EMBASSIES, HEALTH AND MEDICAL CARE, POLICE, TRAVEL PHONE)

Dial 110 for police, 119 for an ambulance or the fire brigade. In case of illness, you should notify the hotel desk immediately.

Call the police.	警察を呼んでください。	keisatsu o yonde kudasai
Get help quickly.	すぐに助けを呼んでください。	sugu ni tasuke o yonde kudasai
Get a doctor.	医者を呼んでください。	isha o yonde kudasai
Help!	助けて！	tasukete
I'm lost!	道に迷いました。	michi ni mayoimashita

GETTING TO JAPAN   G

From Great Britain. Daily flights run to Tokyo from London Heathrow. Non-stop flights take 12 hours, otherwise about 20 hours. The cheapest fare is Apex: the flight must be booked a month in advance, for stays from 14 days to 3 months, with no stopovers.

From North America. There are several daily non-stop flights from New York (15 hours), Los Angeles and San Francisco, and many other cities. Round-the-world fares are available, which allow flights to Europe from North America, then on to the Far East, returning directly to North America. This fare is designed for those who wish to stop en route in Europe. Apex advance booking is available, and cheaper fares exist for groups (minimum 10 people).

From Australia. Direct flights run daily from Sydney to Tokyo, taking about 9 hours.

GUIDES AND INTERPRETERS （ガイド・通訳）
The Japan National Tourist Organization (JNTO) has inaugurated a "goodwill guide" service. These voluntary guides can easily be recognized by their distinctive badge and will be happy to answer questions and give directions.

If you need a professional guide for sightseeing or for shopping, you can contact major travel agents or the Japan Guides Association:

Shin-Kokusai Bldg., 3-4-1 Marunouchi, Chiyoda-ku, Tokyo; tel. (03)3213-2706.

This organization can provide English-, French-, Spanish-, German-, Chinese-, Italian-, Portuguese- or Russian-speaking guides.

H HAIRDRESSERS AND BARBERS （美容院・理髪店）

Japanese barbershops and hairdressers are renowned for their excellent service. The hotel hairdressers are used to "non-Japanese" hair. If you ask the barber for *"futsu no yo ni"* ("as usual") you will be given a beneficial massage of the head and neck, lasting about an hour. Ladies' hairdressers usually close on Tuesdays and barbers on Mondays; both are open all day Sunday.

I want a haircut, please.	散髪、お願いします。	sanpatsu, onegai shimasu
Don't cut it too short.	余り短く刈らないでください。	amari mijikaku karanai de kudasai
I want a shampoo and set.	シャンプーとセットをお願いします。	shanpū to setto o o-negai shimasu

HEALTH AND MEDICAL CARE

For minor ailments, your hotel can contact an English-speaking doctor. In case of serious illness or accident, you can ask to be taken to a hospital with English-speaking staff, such as St. Lukes International Hospital, Tokyo, or the International Catholic Hospital, Tokyo. In Yokohama, contact the Bluff Hospital, in Kyoto the Japanese Baptist Hospital, in Osaka the Sumitomo Hospital, and in Kobe the Kaisai Hospital.

You will find a large selection of imported medicines and toiletries in the American Pharmacy in Tokyo:

Hibiya Park Bldg. 1, 1-chome Yuraku-cho, Chiyoda-ku, tel. (03) 3271-4034

but much more expensive than back home. If you have special medical needs, you should bring an ample supply with you. Japanese pharmacies are called *yakkyoku; kampoyakkyoku* sell Chinese traditional herbal remedies.

If you are in urgent need of a dentist, you can call at the Oyama Dental Clinic:

B1, Hotel New Otani Arcade, 4-1, Kioicho, Chiyoda-ku, Tokyo, tel. (03)3221-4182.

HOURS (see also COMMUNICATIONS)

Banks: Open 9 a.m. to 3 p.m. weekdays, but now closed every Saturday and Sunday.

Hairdressers: Open 9 a.m. to 8 p.m. every day, except closing day: Monday for barbers, Tuesday for hairdressers.

Museums: Open from 9 a.m. to 4.30 p.m. but closed on Mondays.

Principal businesses: Open 9 a.m. to 5 p.m. weekdays; some open on Saturdays from 9 a.m. to noon; closed on Sundays.

Shops: Open 10 a.m. to 8 p.m. every day. Department stores open 10 a.m. to 7 p.m. daily (closed one weekday).

Temples: Open to visitors from 8 a.m. to 4.30 p.m.

LANGUAGE   L

The Japanese language is totally unrelated to any other oriental language, and profoundly different from English; not only are the words and sentence construction different, but also the whole Japanese way of thinking.

Written Japanese is a combination of three systems: the *kanji*, adopted from the Chinese, are the basic ideograms, each character representing one word; *hiragana* and *katakana* scripts represent individual syllables. *Hiragana* characters are used for words of Japanese origin and for particles (which designate subject or object) added to *kanji,* and *katakana* are used to spell out foreign words and names—a kind of shorthand system. If you look closely at the Japanese characters in this book, you will see the difference between the square *kanji* and the more rounded, flowing *hiragana* and *katakana*.

Grammatical rules are quite simple; there is a rigid rule for word order—subject, object, verb. There are no articles and plurals, no personal pronouns, no forms to indicate person or number, and only two tenses, present and past. Matters are complicated by the adjectives, which have tenses and moods as if they were verbs.

The phrases given in this book are transliterated according to a system called the "Hepburn Romanization"; most of the letters are pronounced as in English, although you should note the following:

- a dash over a vowel means that the sound is lengthened, as if it were pronounced twice
- when consonants are doubled, they should both be pronounced

- there is no stress; the phrase should be pronounced in the same rather monotonous tone
- **g** is pronounced as in English **g**o at the beginning of a word, and as **ng** in ri**ng** everywhere else
- **r** is pronounced with the tongue in the position for **l**
- **s** is always hard as in see

The Berlitz phrase book JAPANESE FOR TRAVELLERS covers most of the situations you are likely to encounter in Japan.

Do you speak English?	英語を話しますか。	eigo o hanashimasu ka
Please	どうぞ。	dōzo
Thank you	ありがとう。	arigato
Yes	はい。	hai
No	いいえ。	iie

LOST PROPERTY （遺失物）

The Japanese are so honest that if you lose something you can be sure that it will be taken to the local Lost and Found Office. Three to five days after it has been handed in, property is sent to the Central Lost and Found Office of the Metropolitan Police:

1-9-11, Koraku, Bunkyo-ku, Tokyo; tel. (03)3814-4151.

Property left in a train is handed in at the Japan Railways Lost and Found Office at Tokyo Station, tel. (03)3231-1880, or at Ueno Station, tel. (03)3841-8069; and if you leave something in a taxi, call the Tokyo Taxi Kindaika Centre, (03)3648-0300.

I've lost my . . . wallet/handbag/ passport	私は財布/ハンドバッグ/ パスポートを失くしました。	watashi wa saifu/ handobaggu/ pasupoto o nakushi mashita

M MAPS

The JNTO provides free tourist maps of Japan, Tokyo, Kyoto, Fuji, Osaka and Hokkaido in English. A road map of Japan has been published in English by Buyodo Co., which can be found in main bookshops.

The maps in this book were prepared by Falk Verlag, Hamburg, who also publish a street map of Tokyo.

MEETING PEOPLE

Japanese society is very formal, and people prefer to be introduced through others rather than initiate a conversation with a stranger. No-one is likely to accost you in the street and invite you into his home, although anyone really eager to practise English may come up to you and spontaneously offer to help. If you know anyone Japanese at home, you can tell them that you intend to go to Japan and they may put you in touch with friends or relations. The JNTO, through their Home Visit System, can arrange for up to four or five people to spend an hour with a Japanese family in their home. These visits take place in 12 cities; you need to give a few days' advance notice in person (not by phone or letter) to the JNTO office in Tokyo or in Kyotó, or to the local application offices in the other areas (addresses available from JNTO). This hospitality is free of charge and visits usually take place after Japanese dinner time (7.30 p.m.).

MONEY MATTERS （通貨）

The monetary system is based on the yen (abbreviated ¥). Coins come in denominations of ¥1, 5, 10, 50, 100 and 500, and banknotes in denominations of ¥500, 1,000, 5,000 and 10,000. A ¥10 or ¥100 coin is useful for public phone boxes, the ¥50 and ¥100 coins for bus tickets, cigarette machines and other vending machines, and for short distance railway tickets.

Banks, currency exchange. When you enter a bank, you will be greeted by someone who will lead you to the appropriate window. You will be invited to sit down while the transaction is being completed; this may take as long as 15 minutes. Your name will be called when your money is ready. Most banks have a special foreign exchange section where foreign cash and traveller's cheques may be exchanged for yen. You must present your passport. Traveller's cheques and international credit cards are accepted by hotels, *ryokan* and stores.

I want to change some dollars/ pounds.	ドル/ポンドを替えたいのですが。	doru/pondo o kaetai no desu ga
Where can I cash a traveller's cheque?	トラベラーチェックをどこで現金に替えられますか。	toraberā cheku o doko de genkin ni kaeraremasu ka

N NAMES

According to Japanese practice, the surname comes first. You should use the suffix -san (Mr., Mrs. or Miss) after the family name. This means that if you meet someone called Horiba Iwao you should address him as "Horiba-san".

Visiting cards. The exchange of cards is the Japanese equivalent of the Western custom of shaking hands: essential to anyone on a business trip. Visiting cards *(meishi)* can be obtained rapidly (printed on one side in English and on the other in Japanese) in most major hotels. Make clear what your position is or it will be assumed to be a lowly one.

NEWSPAPERS AND MAGAZINES （新聞・雑誌）

Foreign magazines, newspapers and books can be found in large bookshops and hotels. Several newspapers are published in English: the *Asahi Evening News,* the *Mainichi Daily News,* the *Japan Times* and *The Daily Yomiuri,* which are on sale in hotels and in newspaper kiosks.

Where can I buy an English-language newspaper?	英字新聞はどこで 買えますか。	Eiji shinbun wa doko de kae masu ka

P PHOTOGRAPHY

This is one of Japan's most flourishing industries. The professional will be delighted by the abundance of sophisticated equipment available, and even the most amateur of photographers should obtain good results in this "photogenic" country. Be careful not to overexpose your photos: the light is strong, especially in spring and autumn.

You will have to obtain permission to photograph Buddhist or Shintoist priests at prayer, and it is forbidden to take photos in museums or during *kabuki* or *bunraku* theatre performances.

POLICE （警察） (see also EMERGENCIES and LOST PROPERTY)

There are small police stations or police boxes *(koban)* on most busy street corners. The police wear a dark blue uniform with a peaked cap; they are extremely courteous and will be ready to help you at any time. You should always present your passport when dealing with the police.

PRICES

To give you an idea of what to expect, here's a list of average prices in Japanese yen (¥). However, they can only be approximate, as inflation creeps relentlessly up, here as elsewhere.

Airport transfer. Narita to Tokyo City Air Terminal (coach): ¥2,700. Narita to Tokyo Station (JR Narita Express): ¥2,890. Narita to Keisei Ueno Station (skyliner): ¥1,740. Narita to Haneda (coach): ¥2,900. Narita to Yokohama City Air Terminal (coach): ¥3,300.

Car hire. ¥8,000–¥15,000 per day. Weekly and monthly rates are also available.

Cigarettes. Japanese: ¥220–¥240; European: ¥350.

Guide. Half day ¥15,000; full day ¥25,000.

Hairdresser. Hotel barbers: haircut: ¥3,500; shave: ¥2,600; shampoo: ¥2,900. City barbers slightly cheaper.

Hotels (double room with bath). *Western style,* per room per day: ¥8,000–¥35,000 (breakfast ¥1,500; lunch ¥3,000; dinner ¥7,000–¥15,000; plus service charge). *Ryokan* (including 2 meals, per person): ¥8,000–¥20,000 per day. Lunch ¥1,000–2,000. *Minshuku* (including 2 meals): ¥5,000–¥6,000 per day.

If the total amount of the bill exceeds ¥5,000 per person per day, a 6% tax is added, after deducting ¥2,000. A service charge of 10% is added to hotel and restaurant bills.

Meals. In a moderate restaurant, a Western meal, e.g. steak, will cost from ¥5,000 to ¥12,000, and a Japanese course meal from ¥8,000 to ¥15,000. A self-service meal can cost from ¥800 to ¥3,000.

Night clubs. Cover charge for one hour: ¥3,000. Hostess service: ¥30,000–¥60,000 for two hours; which means that an evening's entertainment can cost as much as ¥130,000.

Taxi fares. ¥600 for the first 2 kilometres, ¥90 for each additional 415 m. From 11 p.m. to 5 a.m., the fare is increased by 20%.

Transport. Bus: in towns the minimum fare is ¥120, and in big cities ¥160. Long distance coach e.g. Tokyo–Nagoya (6 hours) ¥5,000; Nagoya–Osaka (3 hrs 20 min) ¥2,600. Subway: ¥120. Rail pass: first-class, ¥37,000 for 7 days, ¥60,000 for 14 days and ¥78,000 for 21 days. Ordinary class: 7 days ¥27,800, 14 days ¥44,200, 21 days ¥56,600. Children from 6 to 11 pay half price.

PUBLIC HOLIDAYS

January 1	New Year's Day
January 15	Adults' Day
February 11	National Foundation Day
March 21	Vernal Equinox Day
April 29	Green Day
May 3	Constitution Day
May 5	Children's Day
September 15	Respect for the Aged Day
September 23	Autumnal Equinox Day
October 10	Health-Sports Day
November 3	Culture Day
November 23	Labour Thanksgiving Day
December 23	Emperor Akihito's Birthday

If a National Holiday falls on a Sunday, the following Monday is counted as a holiday.

If you intend to be in Japan during the Japanese public holidays at New Year or in "Golden Week" (April 29–May 5) or during the school holidays (July and August) you should make your reservations *well* in advance, for hotels are full and public transport is more packed than ever at these times. It may be the ideal moment to visit Tokyo under less crowded conditions, with the exception of New Year when thousands of provincials flock to Tokyo's Imperial Palace Gardens.

R RADIO AND TV
The Far East Network (FEN 810 KHz), maintained by the U.S. military forces stationed in Japan, broadcasts radio programmes in English. All television programmes are in Japanese, although major hotels in Osaka and Tokyo have some English-language programmes through cable TV.

RELIGIOUS SERVICES
Although Shinto and Buddhism are the major religions, there are over 900,000 Christians in Japan, with churches in nearly every town. However, few services are conducted in English. Information on Protestant, Roman Catholic, Greek Orthodox, Russian Orthodox, Muslim and Jewish services is given in the English-language newspapers.

236

RESTAURANTS (レストラン)

There are many types of eating and drinking places, with a wide variety of foreign and Japanese food. Some restaurants specialize in certain dishes, for example, *sukiyaki* restaurants, *tempura* restaurants, etc. Here you will get good value for money, if you ask for the speciality.

A **bar** *(ba)* serves snacks and drinks.

In a **beer garden** *(biyagaden),* on the rooftops of downtown buildings, you can obtain beer and snacks (open in July and August).

The **coffee shop** *(kissaten)* is the most common establishment, where you can ask for coffee, soft drinks, snacks such as toast, sandwiches, pastries, ice-cream. The coffee is good and strong; for a milder blend, you should ask for "American".

A **sake bar** *(nomiya)* serves the famous Japanese rice wine, but also beer, appetizers and Japanese snacks.

A **restaurant** *(restoran)* may serve foreign food, e.g. French, Chinese, etc., or Japanese or Japanized Western-style food. A *ryoriya* specializes in Japanese food, and can contain an *ozashiki* (private room) where the meal is served in your own Japanese-style room; a counter restaurant where your dish will be prepared in front of you, and a table service. Prices are not always displayed, but some of these restaurants present plastic models of the dishes in the window, showing the price and bearing a number. You should tell the cashier the number (or write it down).

There are very economical and convenient restaurants in large department stores, concert and conference halls and in shopping centres. Some of these work on a "meal ticket" system—the cashier at the door will ask you to buy a ticket on entering. When you sit down, a waiter or waitress will come and pick up your ticket and then fetch your food. Other economical restaurants are situated in the basement of large buildings, where Japanese office workers dine between 12 and 1 p.m. There are clusters of inexpensive restaurants in back streets, and many fast-food chains.

At lunch time on week days, restaurants offer a set menu. This is much cheaper than evening prices and usually consists of salad, soup, main course and coffee.

Breakfast is served until 10 a.m.; lunch from noon to 2 p.m.; and dinner from 6 p.m. to 9 p.m.

If your bill comes to more than ¥2,500, you will have to pay 10 percent tax, and some restaurants add 10–15 percent service charge.

Good evening. I'd like a table for three.	今晩は。3人用のテーブルはありますか。	konbanwa, san-nin-yō no tēburu wa arimasu ka
Could we have a table by the window?	窓の側のテーブルがいいのですが。	mado no soba no tēburu ga ii no desu ga
What's the price of the fixed menu?	今日の定食はいくらですか。	kyō no teishoku wa ikura desu ka

S SHOPPING (see also pp. 201–206)

Japan is a veritable paradise for shoppers, provided that you avoid the dishonest touts on street corners: department stores are open Saturdays and Sundays, and even on holidays (one weekday closing); souvenir shops are open 7 days a week. There are many "cut-price" shops where you can save from 5–40%, and if you are willing to fill in lengthy forms you can obtain tax exemption when you see a "tax-free" sign (you will need to produce your passport). You will find detailed information about sales in the English-language newspapers. Most shops have an information desk near the entrance, with a list of items sold on each floor, and a woman positioned near the escalators to answer inquiries. Most of the staff speak English.

In 1989, a consumption tax was introduced, with 3% added to nearly all goods and services upon purchase.

T TIME DIFFERENCES

Japan is 9 hours ahead of Greenwich Mean Time year-round. The chart below refers to the period March/April to September/October, when many countries move their clocks one hour ahead.

New York	London (GMT + 1)	**Tokyo**	Sydney
7 a.m.	noon	**8 p.m.**	9 p.m.

What time is it?	いま何時ですか。	ima nanji desu ka

TIPPING

It is not customary to tip, and the practice is discouraged by the authorities. Porters at the airport and in the railway stations charge a set fee. A service charge is added to hotel and restaurant bills. However, a small gift may be an appreciated gesture (e.g.

a souvenir of your home town) for people who have been extremely helpful. It is considered courteous to refuse gifts once or twice.

TOILETS （トイレ）

Public toilets are scarce: use those in the department stores. These are generally Western-style, as are those in the big hotels. Japanese-style toilets are level with the floor and have no seats; you have to squat, facing the flushing handle. Usually the door will lock, but it is customary to give two taps on the door to see if the toilet is occupied. If you are inside, you should give two taps back. Many public toilets are shared by men and women; the men at urinals are supposed to be ignored. Toilets are kept scrupulously clean. You should always carry tissues with you.

Where are the toilets?	手洗はどこですか。	te-arai wa doko desu ka
Ladies	女子用	joshi-yō
Gentlemen	男子用	danshi-yō

TOURIST INFORMATION OFFICES （観光案内所）

The JNTO (Japan National Tourist Organization) is a central body to promote and develop the tourist industry. It is a non-profit organization subsidized by the government under the supervision of the Ministry of Transport, and operates Tourist Information Centers (TIC), where you can obtain maps, information, tour itineraries and advice on transport. For information on major events and entertainment in and around Tokyo, you can use the Teletourist service; dial (03)3503-2911.

JNTO Head office in Japan:

10-1, Yurakucho 2-chome, Chiyoda-ku, Tokyo.

TIC Tokyo office:

Kotani Bldg., 1-6-6 Yurakucho, Chiyoda-ku, Tokyo; tel. (03)3502-1461.

New Tokyo International Airport office:

Airport Terminal Bldg., Narita, Chiba Pref. 286-11; tel. (0476) 32-8711.

Kyoto office:

Kyoto Tower Bldg., Higashi-Shiokojicho, Shimogyo-ku, Kyoto; tel. (075)371-5649.

Overseas offices:

Australia: 115 Pitt St., Sydney, N.S.W. 2000; tel. 232-4522.

Canada: 165 University Ave., Toronto, Ont. M5H 3B8; tel. (416)366-7140.

U.K.: 167 Regent St., London W.1; tel. 734-9638.

U.S.A.: 630 Fifth Ave., New York, N.Y. 10111; tel. (212)757-5640.

See also TRAVEL PHONE.

Where is the Tourist Information Centre?	ツーリスト・インフォメーション・センターはどこですか。	tsū risuto info mēshon sentā wa doko desu ka

TRANSPORT

Taxis. They are readily available at hotels, stations and airports, and can be flagged down at street corners, except in certain locations, e.g. the Ginza, where they stop only at authorized taxi ranks. They are bright yellow or green and have a lamp on the roof. If the lamp behind the windscreen is red, saying *kusha,* the taxi is free; a green light means that it is occupied. The doors are remote-controlled by the driver. As few taxi drivers speak English, it is wise to have your destination written down on a piece of paper. After 11 o'clock at night, many taxi drivers in Tokyo prefer more lucrative custom than hotel-bound foreigners and do not stop. If you have a problem, ask a Japanese to hail a taxi for you.

Subway. A dozen subway lines criss-cross Tokyo and are more practical than buses for visiting the city. You have to buy a ticket from a vending machine or from a ticket counter and show it at the gate, where it will be punched. When you reach your destination you will have to hand it in. The station platform signs are in large Japanese and Roman letters. The smaller letters at the bottom of the sign indicate the previous and following stations. It is best to avoid the rush hours, 7 to 9 a.m. and 5 to 7 p.m.

Bus. A complicated network of buses connects most areas of the large cities. In Kyoto and Nagoya this is a very useful and economical means of transport, but in Tokyo it is easier to take the subway. The buses are usually one-man operated; the driver will tell you the fare, which you should put in a box by his seat. In some cities you pay when you get off the bus. Carry several ¥10 and 100 coins with you as the driver may not have change.

Trains. The railway network covers the whole country; it is reputed to be clean, safe and punctual. The world-famous super express *shinkansen* has one westbound and two recently-opened northbound lines. The westbound one, called Gokaido-Sanyo shinkansen, offers two kinds of service: the *hikari* stops only at major stations and the *kodama* stops at every station. There are three other types of train: the limited express *(tokkyu)* for long-distance travel, the ordinary express *(kyuko)* for medium-distance travel, and local trains *(futsu)* for short distances. First-class carriages are called "green cars" *(greensha)*, marked with a green four-leaf sign. Tourists can obtain special rail passes which provide unlimited travel on the Japan Railways, buses and ferries throughout Japan. These passes must be obtained *outside* Japan, from offices of Japan Air Lines, from travel agents or from Japan Travel Bureau offices.

Domestic Flights. Three main air companies assure regular liaison flights between the biggest Japanese cities: Japan Air Lines, All Nippon Airways and Toa Domestic Airlines.

I'd like a ticket to ...	···までの切符を 買いたいのですが。	... made no kippu o no desu ga
single (one-way)	片道	kata michi
return (round-trip)	往復	ō fuku
I'd like a taxi.	タクシーに乗りたい のですが。	takushii ni noritai no desu ga

TRAVEL PHONE

This system has been devised by the Japan National Tourist Organization to help tourists in difficulty, in need of guidance or information or with language problems. An English-speaking travel expert replies every day from 9 a.m. to 5 p.m. You should dial the following numbers, from the yellow or blue public phones or from a private phone.

Tokyo area: 3502-1461
Kyoto area: 371-0480 (charge: ¥10 for 3 minutes).

Elsewhere, the Travel Phone service is free. Insert a ¥10 coin, which will be returned after the call.

Eastern Japan: 0120-222-800
Western Japan: 0120-444-800

W WATER （飲料水）

Tap water is clean and potable everywhere in Japan.

WEIGHTS AND MEASURES

All the ancient measures have been abolished in favour of the metric system, apart from specific measures for kimono-making or for carpentry in Shintoist temples.

Temperature

°C	30	25	20	15	10	5	0	5	10	15	20	25	30	35	40	45
°F	-20	-10	0	10	20	30	40	50	60	70	80	90	100	110		

Length

cm	0		5		10		15		20		25		30
inches	0		2		4		6		8		10		12

metres	0				1 m						2 m
ft./yd.	0		1 ft		1 yd.				2 yd.		

Weight

grams	0	100	200	300	400	500	600	700	800	900	1 kg
ounces	0	4	8	12	1 lb.	20	24	28	2 lb.		

Fluid measures

imp.gals.	0				5					10
litres	0	5	10		20		30		40		50
U.S.gals.	0			5			10			

Kilometres to miles

km	0	1	2	3	4	5	6	8	10	12	14	16
miles	0	½	1	1½	2	3	4	5	6	7	8	9	10

Y YOUTH HOSTELS

Public youth hostels are operated by national or regional governments, and privately run youth hostels are affiliated to the Japan Youth Hostels Inc. (JYH). You need a membership card of a Youth Hostel Association of your home country, or an International Guest Card obtainable from JYH. Reservations should be made directly to individual hostels in writing, within 90 days of your arrival, stating name, address, occupation, sex, membership card number, length of stay, arrival and departure dates, and meal requirements the day you arrive; and you should include two international reply coupons. The booking form is available from the International Youth Hostel Federation (IHYF). Further information can be obtained from JYH Inc.:

3rd floor Hoken Kaikan Bldg.; 1-2 Ichigaya-Sadoharacho, Shinjuku-ku, Tokyo 162; tel. (03)3269-5831.

USEFUL EXPRESSIONS

Please.	どうぞ。	dōzo
Thank you.	ありがとう。	arigatō
Yes/No.	はい／いいえ。	hai /iie
Excuse me.	すみません。	sumimasen
Help me, please.	手助けをお願いします。	tedasuke o onegai shimasu
I don't understand.	わかりません。	wakari ma sen
Do you speak English?	英語を話しますか。	eigo o hanashi masu ka
Where is the consulate?	領事館はどこですか。	ryō ji kan wa doko desu ka
American	アメリカの	ame rika
Australian	オーストラリアの	ō suto raria no
British	イギリスの	igi risu no
Canadian	カナダの	kanada no
New Zealand	ニュージーランド	nyū jii ran do
Good morning.	おはようございます。	ohayō gozai masu
Good evening.	こんばんは。	kon ban wa
Good night.	おやすみなさい。	oyasumi nasai
Goodbye.	さようなら。	sayonara
How are you?	こんにちは。	kon nichi wa
Very well, thank you.	わかりました。ありがとう。	wakari mashita, ari ga tō
And you?	あなたはどうですか。	anata wa dou desu ka
good/bad	よい／悪い	yoi/waru i
big/small	大きい／小さい	ōki i/chiisa i
cheap/expensive	安い／高い	yasui/takai
near/far	近い／遠い	chikai/to o i
old/new	古い／新しい	furui/atarashi i
old/young	年配／若い	nenpai/wakai
beautiful/ugly	きれい／醜い	kirei/minikui

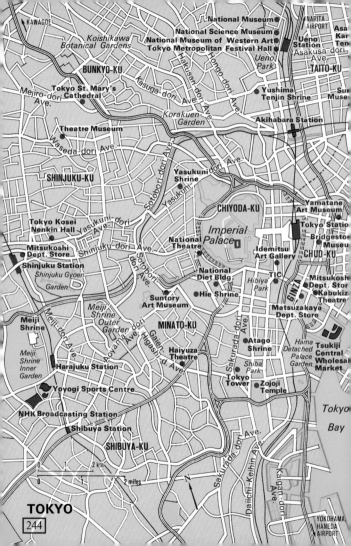

TOKYO

244

TOKYO SUBWAY

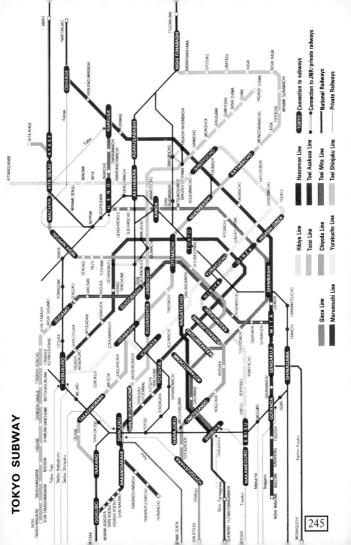

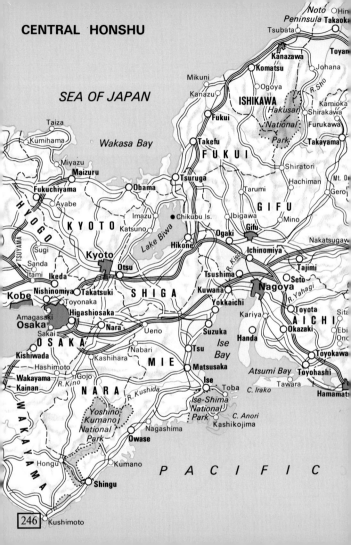

O C E A N

Izu Islands

KYOTO

0   500   1000   1500 m
0   500   1000   1500 yards

N

Midorogaike Pond
Takaragaike Pond

River Kamo

Shugakuin Imperial Vill.

Kitayama-dori Av.

Kitayama-dori Av.

River Takano

Horikawa-dori Av.

Botanical Gardens

Shisendo Temple

Daitokuji Temple

Kinkakuji Temple

Kitaoji-dori Av.

Funaoka Park

Sembon-dori Av.

Nishioji-dori Av.

RYOANJI

SAGA, SEIRYUJI TEMPLE

Myorenji Temple

Myokenji Temple

Shokokuji Temple

Shimogamo-dori Av.

Demachi-Yanagi Sta.

Chionji Temple

Shisendo Temple

Kitano Shrine

Imadegawa-dori Av.

Nishijin Textile Museum

Kyoto Old Imperial Palace

Imperial Park

Imadegawa-dori Av.

Yoshida Shrine

Ginkakuji Temple

Kamo Br.

Shinnyodo Temple

Reikanji Temple

Imperial Household Agency

Karasuma-dori Av.

Higashioji-dori Av.

Marutamachi-dori Av.

Shirakawa-dori

Marutamachi-dori Av.

Nijo Castle

Okazaki Park

National Museum of Modern Art

Museum of Traditional Industry

Nanzenji Temple

Shinsen-en Garden

Oike-dori Av.

Sanjo-dori Av.

Sanjo Br.

Sanjo Sanjo-dori Av.

Shoren-in Temple

TENRYUJI TEMPLE, KORYUJI TEMPLE, ARASHIYAMA

Goin Av.

Kawaramachi Station

Minamiza Theatre

Chion-in Temple

Maruyama Park

Shijo-dori Av.

Shijo-dori Av.

Yasaka Shrine

Shijo-Omiya Station

Kaburenjo Theatre (Gion Corner)

Kiyomizu Temple

Omiya-dori Av.

Horikawa-dori Av.

Karasuma-dori Av.

Kawaramachi-dori Av.

Kamo Br.

Gojo-dori Av.

Gojo-dori Av.

SAIHOJI TEMPLE

KATSURA IMPERIAL VILLA

Nishioji-dori

Nishi-Honganji Temple

Higashi-Honganji Temple

Kyoto National Museum

Mt. Kiyomizu

Shichijo-dori Av.

Shichijo-dori Av.

Chishakuin Temple

TIC

Shiokoji-dori Av.

Sanjusangendo Temple

Kyoto Station

Shinkansen

248

Kujo-dori Av.

Kujo-dori Av.

NARA

Shinkansen

Tofukuji Temple

NARA

500 m
500 yards

Nara-Okuyama Driveway

Wakakusayama Hill

Mikasa Spa

Nigatsudo Hall
Sangatsudo (Hokkedo) Hall

Todaiji Temple
(Daibutsu—Great Buddha)

Isuien Garden
Nandaimon Gate
Himuro Shrine

Nara National Museum

Man'yo Botanical Gardens

Kasuga Grand Shrine

Kasuga Wakamiya Shrine

Mt. Kasuga

Shin-Yakushiji Temple

Nara Park

Araike Pond

Sagiike Pond

Kaidan-in Temple

Five-Storey Pagoda

Kofukuji Temple

Sarusawa Pond

Saihoji Temple

Kanoike Pond

Stadium

Dreamland

Pagoda

Kintetsu Nara Sta.

Nara Sta.

Sanjo-dori St.

Ichijo-dori St.

TENRI

KORIYAMA

River Bodai

N

Futaiji Temple

River Saho

Shin-Omiya Sta.

TOSHODAIJI
YAKUSHIJI
HORYUJI

KYOTO

249

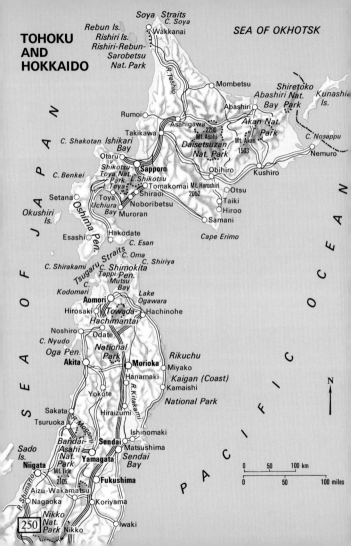

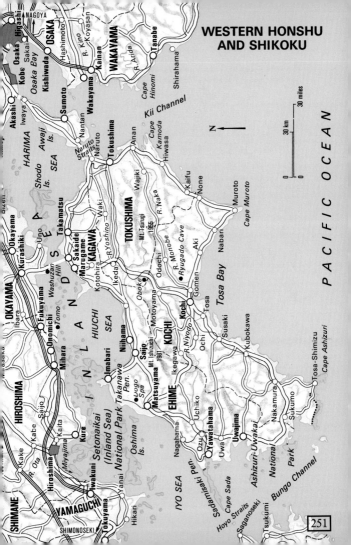

WESTERN HONSHU AND SHIKOKU

PACIFIC OCEAN

N

30 miles
30 km

KYUSHU

252

INDEX

An asterisk (*) next to a page number indicates a map reference. Where there is more than one set of page references, the one in bold type refers to the main entry. For index to Practical Information, see also pp. 218–219.

INDEX

INDEX